Understanding
THE HUMAN BODY

The Immune System

Titles in the Understanding the Human Body series include:

The Brain and Nervous System

The Circulatory System

The Digestive System

The Immune System

The Reproductive System

The Respiratory System

Understanding
THE HUMAN BODY

The Immune System

Pam Walker and Elaine Wood

LUCENT
BOOKS ®

THOMSON
———※———™
GALE

San Diego • Detroit • New York • San Francisco • Cleveland • New Haven, Conn. • Waterville, Maine • London • Munich

© 2003 by Lucent Books. Lucent Books is an imprint of The Gale Group, Inc.,
a division of Thomson Learning, Inc.

Lucent Books® and Thomson Learning™ are trademarks used herein under license.

For more information, contact
Lucent Books
27500 Drake Rd.
Farmington Hills, MI 48331-3535
Or you can visit our Internet site at http://www.gale.com

LIBRARY OF CONGRESS CATALOGING-IN-PUBLICATION DATA

Walker, Pam, 1958–
    The Immune System / by Pam Walker and Elaine Wood.
        p. cm. — (Understanding the human body)
Summary: Describes the structure and function of the immune system and discusses
allergies, autoimmune disease, and vaccines.
Includes bibliographical references and index.
    ISBN 1-59018-151-4
    1. Immune system—Juvenile literature. [1. Immune system.] I. Wood, Elaine, 1950– II.
Title. III. Series.
    QR181.8 .W35 2003
    616.07'9—dc21

                    2002000452

Printed in the United States of America

CONTENTS

FOREWORD   6

CHAPTER ONE
Structure of the Immune System   8

CHAPTER TWO
The Immune System at Work   25

CHAPTER THREE
Allergies: False Alarms
for the Immune System   41

CHAPTER FOUR
Autoimmune Diseases: When
the Body Attacks Itself   53

CHAPTER FIVE
Using Medical Technologies   68

Glossary   84

For Further Reading   86

Works Consulted   88

Index   91

Picture Credits   96

About the Authors   96

FOREWORD

Since Earth first formed, countless creatures have come and gone. Dinosaurs and other types of land and sea animals all fell prey to climatic shifts, food shortages, and myriad other environmental factors. However, one species—human beings—survived throughout tens of thousands of years of evolution, adjusting to changes in climate and moving when food was scarce. The primary reason human beings were able to do this is that they possess a complex and adaptable brain and body.

The human body is comprised of organs, tissue, and bone that work independently and together to sustain life. Although it is both remarkable and unique, the human body shares features with other living organisms: the need to eat, breathe, and eliminate waste; the need to reproduce and eventually die.

Human beings, however, have many characteristics that other living creatures do not. The adaptable brain is responsible for these characteristics. Human beings, for example, have excellent memories; they can recall events that took place twenty, thirty, even fifty years earlier. Human beings also possess a high level of intelligence. Their unique capacity to invent, create, and innovate has led to discoveries and inventions such as vaccines, automobiles, and computers. And the human brain allows people to feel and respond to a variety of emotions. No other creature on Earth has such a broad range of abilities.

Although the human brain physically resembles a large, soft walnut, its capabilities seem limitless. The brain controls the body's movement, enabling humans to sprint, jog, walk, and crawl. It controls the body's internal functions, allowing people to breathe and maintain a heartbeat without effort. And it controls a person's creative talent, giving him or her the ability to write novels, paint masterpieces, or compose music.

Like a computer, the brain runs a network of body systems that keep human beings alive. The nervous system relays the brain's messages to the rest of the body. The respiratory system draws in life-sustaining oxygen and expels carbon dioxide waste. The circulatory system carries that oxygen to and from the body's vital organs. The reproductive system allows humans to continue their species and flourish as the dominant creatures on the planet. The digestive system takes in vital nutrients and converts them into the energy the body needs to grow. And the immune system protects the body from disease and foreign objects. When all of these systems work properly, the result is an intricate, extraordinary living machine.

Even when some of the systems are not working properly, the human body can often adapt. Healthy people have two kidneys, but, if necessary, they can live with just one. Doctors can remove a defective liver, heart, lung, or pancreas and replace it with a working one from another body. And a person blinded by an accident, disease, or birth defect can live a perfectly normal life by developing other senses to make up for the loss of sight.

The human body adapts to countless external factors as well. It sweats to cool off, adjusts the level of oxygen it needs at high altitudes, and derives nutritional value from a wide variety of foods, making do with what is available in a given region.

Only under tremendous duress does the human body cease to function. Extreme fluctuations in temperature, an invasion by hardy germs, or severe physical damage can halt normal bodily functions and cause death. Yet, even in such circumstances, the body continues to try to repair itself. The body of a diabetic, for example, will take in extra liquid and try to expel excess glucose through the urine. And a body exposed to extremely low temperatures will shiver in an effort to generate its own heat.

Lucent's Understanding the Human Body series explores different systems of the human body. Each volume describes the parts of a given body system and how they work both individually and collectively. Unique characteristics, malfunctions, and cutting edge medical procedures and technologies are also discussed. Photographs, diagrams, and glossaries enhance the text, and annotated bibliographies provide readers with opportunities for further discussion and research.

Structure of the Immune System

The human body is designed to take good care of itself. It performs millions of tasks each day to sustain, build, and repair body tissues. Delivery of food and oxygen to cells, generation of energy, removal of waste products, and production of new cells for growth and for replacement of worn out cells are all part of its daily routine. Cellular maintenance and growth are never ending processes in the body.

If humans lived in a world without microorganisms, or where people never get injured, a specialized mechanism for defense and repair would not be needed. However, this is not the case. The human body is constantly subjected to life-threatening conditions. One way the body can be hurt is through an injury. Any injury, whether as minor as a cut in the skin or as serious as a shattered leg bone, interferes with the body's ability to function. The human body can also be hurt by the invasion of microorganisms. Microorganisms are living things that are so small they are invisible to the naked eye. Some examples of microorganisms include bacteria, viruses, protozoans, and some fungi. Microorganisms are everywhere: in the air, water, and soil. Despite their huge population, only a few of these ever invade the human body. Those that do take up residence in the body find it to be an excellent home because it is warm, moist, and full of nutrients. An infection results when microorganisms invade the body and multiply. The body has developed a specialized defense mechanism to protect itself from both physical damage and these parasitic life forms. This remarkable mechanism is called the immune system.

Job Description

The immune system has two basic jobs: to protect the body from invading microorganisms, and to help the body repair injuries. A properly functioning immune system is essential for survival. Despite its immense importance, the immune system is rather inconspicuous. It is not made up of large organs, and none of its features are visible from the outside. Unless they become injured or sick, most people do not even notice their immune systems.

When a microorganism invades the body, it multiplies causing infection and we will frequently seek a doctor's help.

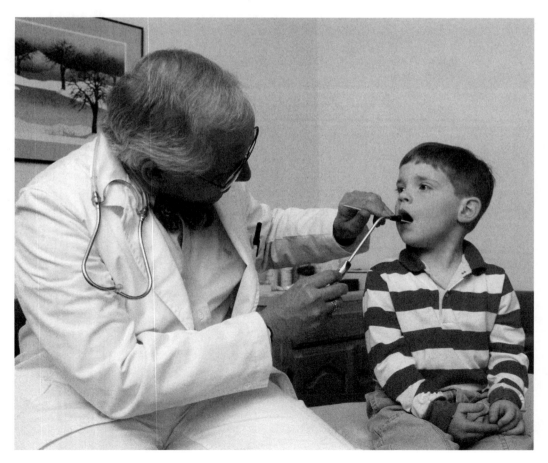

The immune system must be able to launch an attack quickly and efficiently. Consequently it commands an arsenal of impressive weapons. This artillery provides defense on many levels. First, the immune system presents a physical barrier to keep invading cells out of the body. If invaders are able to penetrate this barrier, an array of nonspecific defense armaments, designed to recognize and destroy anything in the body that does not belong there, comes into action. These nonspecific defenses have an excellent record of catching and stopping most invaders. However, if they are overwhelmed by a strong assault, then the "smart" guns are needed: weapons that are able to seek out specific targets. With these weapons, the immune system springs into full action and launches an aggressive campaign to hunt down and destroy intruders.

Before the immune system can wipe out an invader, it must be able to recognize it. This means that the system must have the ability to tell the difference between cells of its own body and foreign materials. In the study of the immune system, body cells are referred to as "self" and foreign cells or objects as "nonself." Every cell that belongs to an individual carries a special label that identifies it as self for that individual. This label is made of molecules that are displayed on the surface of each cell. These identifying molecules are vital; without them the immune system cannot tell which cells belong to the body. Any substance or cell without these identifiers is considered to be nonself and is targeted for destruction.

Cells or substances that are not part of the body, that is, nonself molecules, are called antigens. One critical job of the immune system is to identify antigens, and recognition of such nonself materials is called the immune response. A variety of materials can act as antigens. For example, a bacterium, or even a piece of a bacterium, is seen by the immune system as nonself. Splinters or pieces of dirt that penetrate the skin also register as nonself, or antigenic, substances. Even tissues or cells from other individuals have their own distinctive cell surface molecules, so they are also perceived as antigens.

Foreign materials can enter the body at many points. Therefore, tissues and organs of the immune system are strategically stationed throughout the body. This makes it possible for immune system cells to easily hunt down and destroy invaders wherever they are. Immune system organs are also called lymphoid organs because they are the sites where specialized immune cells, lymphocytes, are produced. Lymphoid organs include the bone marrow, thymus, lymph system, spleen, tonsils, adenoids, appendix, and several clumps of tissues in the digestive system.

Although it is not considered to be an organ of the immune system, skin plays an important role in protecting the

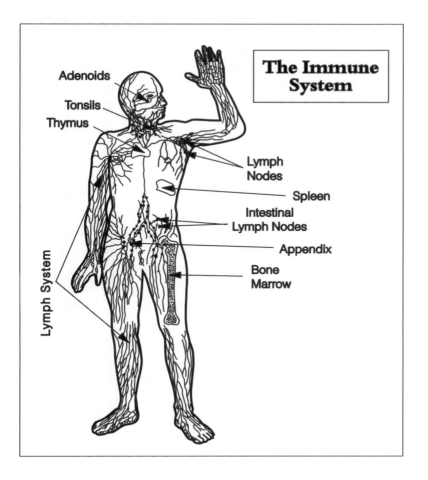

body. Intact skin provides both a physical and a chemical barrier to invaders, a barrier so effective that microorganisms cannot penetrate it. The skin keeps out foreign materials very much like plastic wrap protects food. Whereas the underside of skin continuously divides and grows, the outside layer is made of hardened cells reinforced by a strong waterproof protein called keratin. Older skin cells are constantly being pushed up from the growing layers toward the surface. Here, their nutrient supplies are scarce and they eventually die and are rubbed off.

Guarding the Entries

There are some natural entry points through the skin. The respiratory, digestive, urinary, and reproductive systems all have openings that connect them to the outside environment. At these openings, the body is most vulnerable to attack. The nose and mouth are two places where microbes constantly attempt to invade. To protect itself, the body is equipped with several defenses at all openings to the external environment.

Entry points of the body are guarded by an assortment of nonspecific defenses. For example, hairs in the nose filter dust and large bacteria from air before it enters the body. The nose and other body cavities are lined with mucous membranes. Mucus in the nose and throat traps microbes and dust that gets past the hairs. Mucus, along with tears and saliva, also contains a chemical that can destroy many foreign cells. Cilia, tiny hairlike projections on cells in mucous membranes, sweep mucus out of the throat and windpipe. Any invaders on food are killed by strong acid in the stomach.

Lymph Cells: Soldiers in the Defense Battle

The immune system has a huge arsenal of cells. Some are designed to work in the nonspecific defense program, while others are part of the specific defense army. For the immune system to be effective, all of its cells and organs must work together. To coordinate their efforts, they communicate with each other by direct contact and through chemical messengers. No one kind of cell can take care of every type of invader.

Like all cells, cells of the immune system begin their life in bone marrow. Marrow is the soft tissue in the hollow shafts of long bones. It produces millions of special cells called stem cells that are the precursors to other cell types. The name "stem" was given to cells from bone marrow because they branch out and become a variety of different types of cells.

Collectively, all of the cells of the immune system are called white blood cells or leukocytes. They do their work in blood, lymph, and lymph organs. White blood cells look and behave very differently from other body cells. They are generally large and have the ability to move around like single-celled organisms such as amoeba. White blood cells can be subdivided into three classes: lymphocytes, granulocytes, and monocytes.

Lymphocytes are small white blood cells that are responsible for a lot of the work done by the immune system. Like other cells, all lymphocytes begin as stem cells in bone marrow. However, each type of lymphocyte matures in a different part of the body and is trained for a different job. Lymphocytes are divided into three classes: B cells, T cells, and natural killer cells.

B Cell Lymphocytes

B cells spend their entire early life in the bone marrow. Not only are they produced there, but they mature there. Once fully grown, their job is to travel through the blood and lymph looking for antigens. Although B cells do not have the ability to destroy invaders, they can call in other parts of the immune system by producing special proteins called antibodies. When an antigen enters the body, it wanders freely until it encounters a B cell that recognizes it. For a B cell to recognize an antigen, it must fit that antigen like a key. Once a B cell has identified its antigen, it begins dividing, making more cells like itself. Each of these

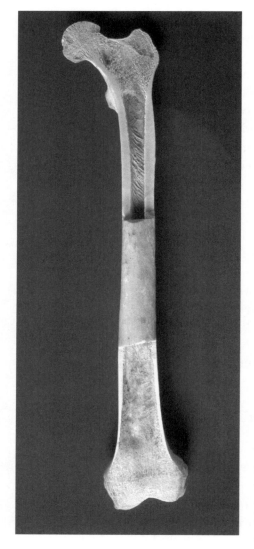

Immune cells begin their lives in the marrow that fills the interior of bones.

cloned B cells matures into a specialized form called a plasma cell. The new plasma cells produce antibodies that aid in neutralizing the antigen that was encountered by the parent B cell. Plasma cells work like high-speed factories, producing more than two thousand antibodies each second. Most of these hardworking cells begin to die after only four or five days. However, a few survive and remain in the body as memory cells, shaped to fit that specific antigen. These cells live for years so that if the body ever needs to produce this particular antibody again, plasma cells can be quickly cloned to fight invaders.

The immune system produces millions of different types of B cells and keeps a few memory cells of each type on hand. Each type of B cell is shaped to match, or recognize, only one antigen. For example, one type of B cell recognizes one of the common cold viruses. When this B cell clones itself and forms plasma cells, all of the resulting antibodies are directed against the one cold virus. A different B cell is capable of identifying streptococci, bacteria that cause strep throat. This B cell clones itself and makes plasma cells which secrete antibodies against the strep throat bacteria. Because specific antibodies fit specific antigens, they can only identify the antigen they match.

Once created and released in the body, antibodies can cause several different immune responses. Some simply bind to antigens, forming a clump called the immune complex. This clump signals the rest of the immune system for help. In response, the immune system sends in cells to consume the entire mass. Other antibodies cover antigens like a coat of paint, making them more attractive to antigen-destroying cells. An alternative effect of antibodies is to draw antigen-destroying chemicals to the site of attack. In the case of viral antigens, antibodies physically prevent them from entering cells. And antibodies made against antigens that are poisons bind to those poisons and disable them. This group of antibodies, which are antitoxins, plays a crucial role in emergency medicine.

T Cell Lymphocytes

Not all lymphocytes mature in the bone marrow like B cells. Some leave the marrow at a very young age and travel to the thymus and mature there. These lymphocytes are called T cells. The thymus is a complex gland that is located in the upper chest between the breastbone and the heart. Its size varies with age. During infancy and childhood, the thymus is relatively large. After puberty it decreases in size; in adults it may be very small. In the elderly, the thymus is absent and in its place are connective and fat tissues.

In the thymus, T cells are imprinted with critically important lessons for distinguishing self and nonself cells. If for some reason a T cell reacts against self tissues, it is destroyed. After the destruction of any such improperly functioning cells, T cells are released to circulate in the blood and lymph. There they have many jobs. Some become cytotoxic T cells. Unlike B cells, they have the ability not only to identify and attach to antigens but also to destroy those that have been labeled as nonself. If necessary, they can attack invaders that have already entered into and infected cells. Sometimes they are able to rid the body of its own cells that have assumed cancerous form by mutating.

Another group of T cells has an entirely different job. They also travel through blood and lymph, looking for invaders. However, when they find one, they do not attack it. Instead, like generals coordinating immune system activities, they notify other parts of the immune system to come help fight the antigen. One way they do this is by secreting chemical messengers known as cytokines. Cytokines have several

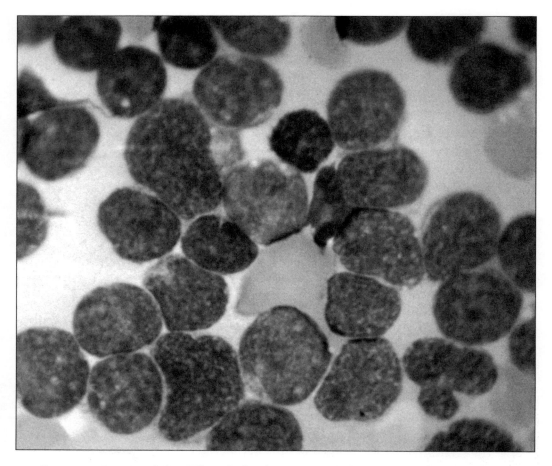

B cells are produced and mature in the bone marrow.

jobs. They help damage and destroy target cells. After the antigens are destroyed, the cytokines stimulate the production of new cells so that tissues can be repaired. One example of a cytokine is interferon, a protein that helps protect cells against viruses.

Natural Killer Cells and Special Forces

Natural killer cells are another type of deadly lymphocyte. Like cytotoxic T cells, they contain lethal chemicals. They are called "natural" killers because, unlike cytotoxic T cells, they are not programmed to recognize a particular antigen. As soon as they are formed, they can destroy both tumor cells and a wide variety of microbes. When a natural killer meets a foreign or tumor cell, it binds to it and releases its chemicals. These chemicals produce a hole in the target cell's membrane, fluids seep in, and the cell bursts.

Many white blood cells can locate, capture, and destroy microbes in a process called phagocytosis. When a phagocytic white blood cell approaches a microbe, it extends a footlike projection of cytoplasm called a pseudopod. Soon the footlike extension surrounds the entire microbe. A phagocytic white blood cell contains an arsenal of deadly chemicals for just such an intruder. Hydrogen peroxide and digestive enzymes are contained in small packages called lysosomes. The cell empties these chemicals onto the captured microbe, killing it.

Granulocytes, Cells with a Different Job

About 50 to 60 percent of the white blood cells in the human body are granulocytes, and every granulocyte is a phagocytic cell containing lysosomes of lethal chemicals.

Like a commanding general, the T cell (center) sends signals to cells to attack and fight invaders.

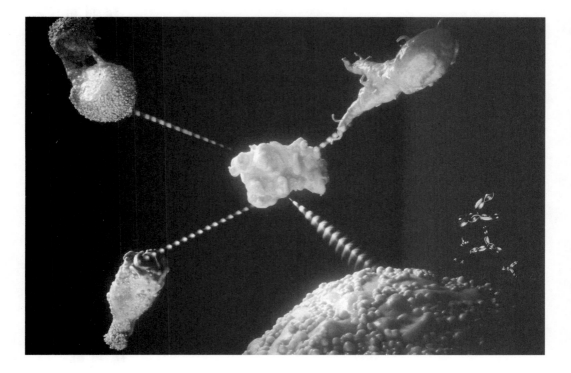

Granulocytes may be neutrophils, eosinophils, or basophils. Neutrophils are by far the most numerous. Although trillions are always present in the body, each lives only a day or two. Neutrophils circulate in the blood. When other immune cells find invaders within body tissues they release chemical messengers. Neutrophils leave the blood to follow these messengers into tissues. On the scene, the neutrophils engulf foreign cells, then kill them with a fatal dose of chemicals. If a lot of foreign cells appear on the scene, thousands of neutrophils travel there and attack each one. As they die, neutrophils, the bacteria that they have killed, and pieces of dead cells form a white semisolid called pus.

The granulocytes called basophils carry histamine, a chemical they release when they find foreign cells. Histamine causes inflammation, which is a good thing from the immune system's point of view. An inflamed area becomes abnormally large and warm, permitting extra blood and lymph fluid to get to the area to deliver other white blood cells and speeding up normal metabolic processes. Inflammation also gets nutrients into and fluids out of the site of attack.

Eosinophils do much of the same kind of work as neutrophils. However, they are not called in to fight infections of viruses and bacteria. Instead, they are activated when the body is infected with parasites, such as roundworms.

Monocytes Become Macrophages

The total white blood cell population consists primarily of lymphocytes and granulocytes; the cells called monocytes make up only about 7 percent of the total. Each monocyte evolves into a type of cell called a macrophage. The "macro" part refers to a large cell, and "phage" means "eater of." These big cells are phagocytes, or cell-eaters, that travel into the tissues. They wander in lymph fluid where they act as scavengers that eat dead cells and disabled antigens. They are important in cleaning up dead neutrophils as part of the healing process.

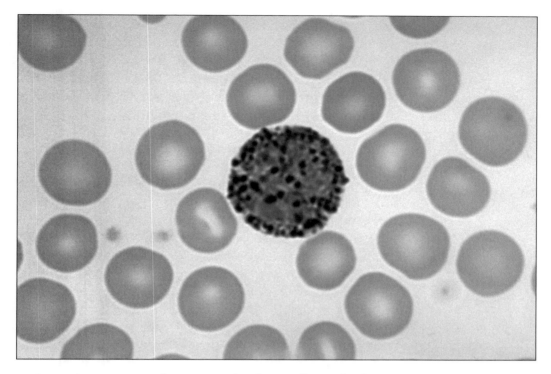

Sometimes macrophages are the first cells to find new antigens in the body. When this happens, they ingest the antigens and display on their surface cell membrane molecules of the new antigens. In this way, macrophages are important in initiating an immune response. They can also activate the group of chemicals called complement proteins. These help cells of the immune system destroy invaders.

Basophils migrate to the site of an injury.

The Complement System

The complement system is composed of a group of twenty proteins that are made by the liver. They float in the bloodstream until they are needed, but move quickly into action when summoned by macrophages, B cells, and others. For example, when a macrophage consumes an antigen, it releases a chemical signal that draws complement proteins to the area. Complement proteins have a variety of roles. They attract more macrophages and neutrophils to the area to consume and destroy antigens. Plus, they aid in clumping, the formation of antibody-antigen complexes. They can also increase the vulnerability of antigens by altering the cell membranes of foreign (nonself) cells, causing them to be easily ruptured. Remarkably, the complement proteins have the ability to change the molecular structure of some viruses, making them harmless.

Lymph and Lymph Nodes

Just in case microorganisms do get past the skin and mucous membranes, nonspecific immune system cells vigilantly patrol the body twenty-four hours a day. They travel along two big highways: the circulatory and the lymph systems. These systems work closely together. Lymph fluid is the clear fluid that makes up most of the blood, but does not contain any of the iron-bearing red blood cells that give blood its characteristic color. Whereas blood is pumped through the body by the heart, the lymph system does not have a pump. Lymph fluids are pushed along their network of vessels by muscle contractions of normal body movements.

One of the jobs of lymph vessels is to gather body fluid that collects in spaces between cells and return that fluid to the bloodstream. The lymph system merges with the circulatory system at a junction in the upper chest near the shoulder. Here large lymph vessels dump their contents into the blood, and the transparent lymph fluid mixes with, and becomes part of, the blood. With the blood, it flows into the right side of the heart, which pumps the mixture back through body tissues. Lymph fluid leaves blood vessels, where it is highly concentrated, and reenters the tissues, where it is scarce, by spreading into spaces between cells.

Another job of the lymph system is to assist in the capture and destruction of invaders or antigens that find their way into the lymph. Clumps of tissues called nodes are located along the lymph vessels. Their job is to filter the lymph fluid during its journey. The small, bean-shaped lymph nodes are less than an inch long. Blood vessels and nerves enter each node at an indented region called the hilum. Each node is en-

closed in a capsule of tough tissue. Lymph nodes strain microbes and other foreign matter out of the blood. Once trapped, this material is destroyed by lymph cells. Lymph nodes are distributed throughout the body to be sure that all invaders are effectively targeted. The largest clusters are found in the neck, armpits, abdomen, and groin. When the body is fighting an invasion of disease-causing microorganisms, lymph nodes swell. When swollen, lymph nodes in the neck can easily be detected by external palpation.

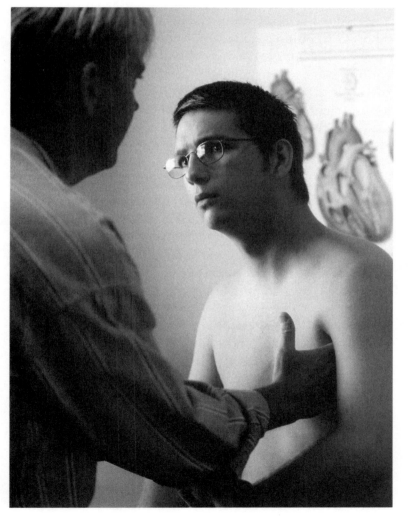

A doctor examines a patient's lymph nodes. Swollen lymph nodes mean the body is fighting infection.

Spleen and Other Lymph Tissue

T cells, B cells, and other immune system cells congregate in lymph tissue throughout the body. One meeting place for many lymph cells is in the spleen, the largest of the lymphoid organs. It is located behind the stomach, above the diaphragm in the upper left section of the abdomen. Blood circulating through the body travels through the spleen. Within this organ are two types of tissue: red pulp and white pulp. The job of red pulp is to remove from circulation red blood cells that have died a natural death. These dead cells are then consumed by scavenger cells. The white pulp is made up of nodules similar to lymph nodes. Microbes carried by the blood get trapped there and immune system cells kill them. People who have had their spleen surgically removed can survive, but they get a lot more colds than people who still possess a spleen. Removal of the spleen can cause serious health problems in children and adults with weak immune systems.

Clumps of lymphoid tissue are found in the gastrointestinal, respiratory, and urogenital tracts. These regions warrant special protection by the immune system because they contain main ports of entry into the body. Areas of tissue called Peyer's patches, located in the intestinal walls, filter out foreign cells that enter the digestive tract. The tonsils also contain a lot of lymphoid tissue and help remove and destroy foreign cells in the upper respiratory system.

Passive and Acquired Immunity

If nonspecific immune defenses such as mucous membranes and macrophages cannot handle an invading antigen, specific immune weapons like B and T cells are called to action. Specific immune cells create immunity, an ability to resist an invader. Immunity can be gained in two ways: passively or actively.

A body gains passive immunity by receiving antibodies from someone else. For example, newborn infants have weak immune systems, possessing only the antibodies received in the womb. Babies who are breastfed receive a boost to their passive immunity because additional antibodies are present in the mother's milk.

A way to gain passive immunity against a particular antigen is by receiving an injection of antibodies. These antibodies must come from the blood of someone who has been infected with and recovered from that particular disease. This type of passive immunity is given to individuals exposed to a serious disease against which they have not been vaccinated.

Active immunity refers to triggering an immune response within the body. This happens when a person is exposed to an antigen naturally or artificially through a vaccine. Active immunity results because the body builds up B cells after its first exposure to an antigen. These B cells produce antibodies to the antigen. After its initial contact with an antigen, the body recovers and most antibody-producing cells die. However, a few are stored as memory cells. The next time contact with the same antigen is made, memory B cells go into action and mount a quick defense.

The Whole Picture

The human body provides a perfect home for many microbes: It is warm and moist, and it supplies plenty of food. However, some microbes can cause disease when they move into the body. The body protects itself by means of the immune system. The immune system's job is to keep out microbes and other cells that do not belong there. If it cannot keep them out, then it hunts them down and destroys them.

The body has developed an elaborate array of cells and chemicals to protect itself. The skin and mucous membranes are equipped to repel invaders when they try to enter the body. If they fail, the lymphatic system takes over. This network of vessels collects fluid from the entire body, then strains it through lymph tissues to remove and destroy invading cells.

If a foreign cell gets past these body defenses, the lymphocytes are called into action. B lymphocytes have the ability to recognize foreign cells but not to destroy them. Instead,

A breast-feeding newborn receives a boost to the immune system from antibodies in the mother's milk.

they create millions of antibody-producing cells. The resulting stream of antibodies identifies the invading organisms so that other immune system cells can destroy them, thus accomplishing the function of the immune system: to protect the body from invasion and damage by microorganisms.

2 The Immune System at Work

A common source of diseases in the human body is infections by bacteria or viruses. Diseases caused by these organisms vary widely in severity, ranging from mild discomfort to life-threatening misery. To protect itself, the body has several lines of defense. If infectious agents are able to get past the skin and mucous membranes, they have to deal with the body's nonspecific defense machinery which, in most cases, can destroy invading microbes. However, a few attackers are able to sneak through this level of security. When this happens, the body declares an all-out war by launching a full immune response, which involves specific defense mechanisms. To accommodate the resulting fight, the body undergoes some dramatic physical changes.

Symptoms of Inflammation

In the war against antigens, the body is a battleground. As such it provides passageways for troops traveling to and from the battle. It also arms these troops and supplies them with nourishment. After a battle, the body removes the corpses of both defenders and invaders, then disposes of all of their fighting equipment.

The condition called inflammation is one of the body's physical adaptations for this battle. Although the immune system works quietly and rarely gets noticed, an inflammatory response can gain attention because an inflamed area may feel uncomfortable or even painful. Inflammation is the

25

body's normal reaction to injury or infection. Just as muscle tissues need extra oxygen and food during periods of intense activity, injured sites require additional immune supplies during infection.

All inflamed areas show one or more of the classic symptoms of inflammation: redness, heat, pain, and swelling. Inflamed tissues often take on a red color. When an injury occurs, the body responds by sending extra blood to the site. Blood is important in the healing process because it carries food and oxygen and removes waste. To accommodate the extra blood, vessels supplying that site enlarge. When the vessels become packed with blood, they give the area a red appearance.

The heat of inflammation is also due to large amounts of blood in the area. Since blood is warm, its increased presence raises the temperature of tissues. Much of the blood that flows to the site of an injury has traveled there from deep inside the body where conditions are warmer than near the surface. In an inflamed area, discomfort can result from an increase in pressure on tissues that are swollen. When sensi-

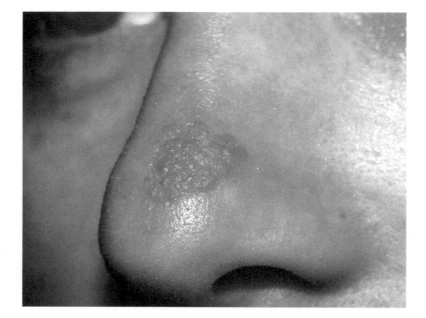

An inflamed area is red, hot, painful, and swollen.

tive nerves are stimulated by swollen tissues, they send signals to the brain, which translates them as pain.

Swelling is due to the supplemental fluid and cells that enter the area of injury. Fluid from blood plasma can seep into the tissues at the site of injury because cells lining the walls of vessels pull back, creating tiny openings in the walls. This makes it easier for fluids and cells to permeate the vessels. White blood cells, especially leukocytes and macrophages, travel through the walls of these blood vessels to the site of injury. They are attracted there by chemicals released from body cells in response to pathogens.

Once inflammation diminishes, tissues begin repairing themselves. In most cases cells divide to make new cells that are identical to the damaged ones. However, injuries that penetrate deeply may leave scars. For example, when injury to skin is deep, cells in its bottom layers speed up their activity so that the damaged tissue can be repaired. Some of this new repair material rises to the top layer of the skin. Scar tissue has a different texture and appearance than normal skin tissue.

Attacking Extracellular Bacteria

Just exactly how the immune system handles an invading antigen depends on the nature of the antigen itself. Trespassers that float around the outside of cells in the spaces between them are relatively easy to destroy. These so-called extracellular antigens are usually bacterial cells.

When extracellular antigens enter the body they encounter the specialized immune cells called macrophages, which consume invaders. For example, when the bacterium *E. coli,* a cause of food poisoning, enters the body, it is devoured by macrophages. This event enables those large white blood cells to alert the immune system to release the cytokines and complement proteins that help destroy other bacteria.

If macrophages are unable to destroy extracellular antigens, the immune system switches to another tactic. In plan B, the immune system traps the invaders within a strong wall of cells called a granuloma. From this prison, the trespassing

Deep injuries can leave scars. Scar tissue is different in texture and appearance from normal skin.

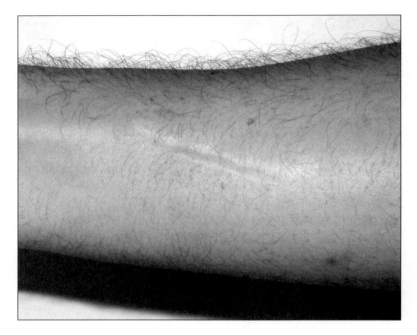

cells cannot damage healthy body cells. The bacteria that cause tuberculosis are good examples of trespassers that are difficult to eliminate. If the immune system fails in its attempts to completely eradicate an infection of tuberculosis bacteria, it erects a wall of cells around the antigens and segregates them from the rest of the body. Over time, the immune system is usually able to destroy the microbes in these granulomas. However, it is possible for the trapped bacteria to become dormant and survive for years. In that case, they can become a source of reinfection.

Encapsulated Extracellular Bacteria

Not all bacteria are as easy to kill as *E. coli*, which lacks a protective coating or capsule. Several types of bacteria are covered, or encapsulated, with thick coatings that prevent macrophages from recognizing these microorganisms as invaders. Therefore, an encapsulated bacterium escapes early capture by patrolling macrophages and travels freely through the body. The bacterium remains unnoticed until it encounters a B cell that is programmed to recognize it. For encapsulated bacteria like the streptococci, B cells are the beginning of the end.

Once a single B cell has identified an intruder, that B cell clones itself into millions of antibody-producing plasma cells. The resulting antibodies bind to the capsules of the invaders. Thus attached, the antibodies and antigens form large units called immune complexes. Immune complexes help eliminate invaders because their presence triggers the complement system, causing complement proteins to flow into the area and attach to the immune complex. An immune complex plus complement constitutes a signal for macrophages to consume the entire structure.

A young patient suffering from an E. coli bacterial infection receives emergency care.

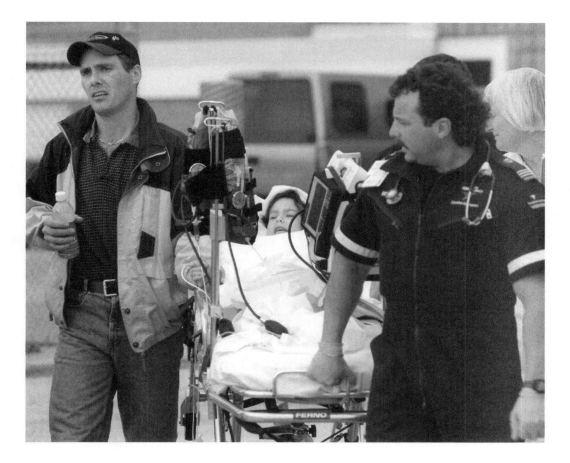

Intracellular Bacteria

Not all bacteria remain in extracellular spaces. Upon entering the body, some head directly for cells and invade them before they are recognized by the immune system. These microorganisms are referred to as intracellular bacteria. When a cell is attacked by bacteria, it strips the enemy microbes of their identifying cell markers and displays them on its membrane. This display is a cry for help by the infected cell to the rest of the immune system. In response, a variety of immune cells flock to the rescue. T cells start the rescue program by releasing cytokines. Cytokines mobilize macrophages which enter the infected area and destroy all the infected cells.

Viruses in Cells

Viruses are another type of antigen that gets into cells. Cells treat viruses very much as they do intracellular bacteria. As soon as the viruses enter a cell, that cell strips off the attacker's surface markers and displays them on its own membrane. Viral markers on cell membranes elicit a slightly different response from the immune system than bacterial markers. They stimulate the production of cytotoxic T cells, and the body needs at least a week to create and mobilize these specialized virus killers. Cytotoxic T cells are very talented because they have the ability to identify and kill only the cells infected with viruses. The influenza virus is an example of a virus that invades body cells and stimulates production of cytotoxic T cells. When T cell production is complete, all infected cells are destroyed. The reason it takes so long to recover from the flu is because it takes seven to ten days to generate enough T cells to consume all the viruses.

When the Body Cannot Respond

Inflammation, release of cytokines and complement proteins, and production of immune cells are all normal parts of the body's immune response. For an immune response to be effective, all parts of the immune system must be func-

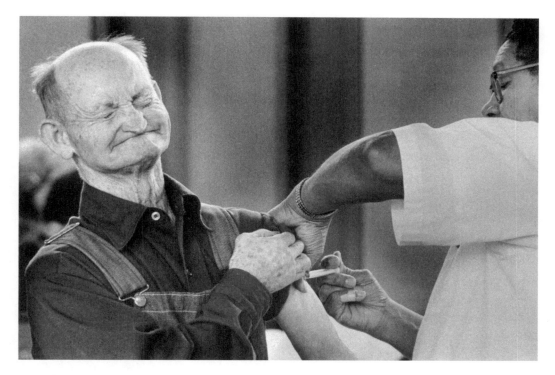

tional. If one part of the system is not working properly the entire system is compromised and may become disabled.

Acquired immunodeficiency syndrome or AIDS epitomizes the ruin of immune system function. The antigen that causes this disease is a virus called HIV, human immunodeficiency virus. Since its identification in Africa in 1981, HIV has traveled across the globe. By the year 2000 the worldwide death toll due to AIDS had reached 21.8 million people. This is about twice the number of soldiers and civilians who were killed in World War II.

Whereas living things can move, gather food, respond to stimuli, grow, and reproduce on their own, viruses cannot carry out any of these functions. They are able to reproduce only when they are inside living cells. Technically, HIV and other viruses are not living things. To establish their presence in a host organism, they must commandeer a living cell's reproductive machinery and use it to make copies of themselves.

Since it takes the body seven to ten days to generate enough T cells to destroy the influenza virus, many people choose to get vaccinated.

How HIV Works

HIV disables the immune system by infecting one type of T cell, the helper T cell. Therefore, when HIV invades the body, it must travel to lymphoid tissue. On its way, it is met by B cells. These watchdogs immediately recognize HIV as an antigen and begin cloning themselves to generate thousands of antibody-producing plasma cells. Three or four weeks after infection, plasma cells have produced enough antibodies to HIV to be detectable in the blood. Blood tests for HIV antibodies form the basis for diagnosing the infection and for screening donated blood. People who have been infected for less than a month usually do not have enough antibodies in their blood to be detected. Unfortunately, antibodies are not able to eliminate the virus, and it continues on its journey. Eventually the virus finds helper T cells and invades them.

Shortly after infection, most people have flulike symptoms for a brief time. They may run a fever, feel tired and

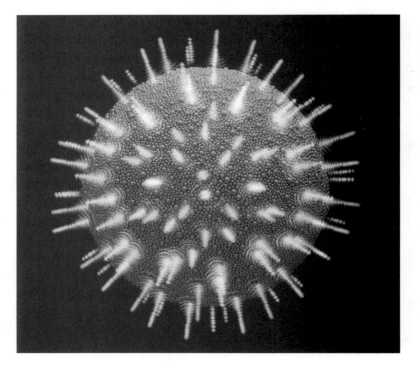

The human immunodeficiency virus, commonly known as HIV, is the antigen that causes AIDS.

achy, and have swollen lymph glands. During this time, HIV is present in large quantities in body fluids and the infected person is very contagious. Most people who experience the early HIV symptoms are unaware of their true condition. Many mistakenly assume that they have the flu or a cold. After two or three weeks, the symptoms disappear.

After the period of early symptoms, HIV can remain hidden in a body for years, and HIV victims may not experience any more indicators of the disease. However, during this time such persons are contagious and can spread HIV to others. Changes occurring within a victim's body are subtle but dangerous. During its residence, HIV continues to seek out, enter, and disable helper T cells. The immune system is unable to stop this process. Defense mechanisms that stop other viruses are ineffective against HIV because it changes forms constantly. Since helper T cells are critical instruments in the body's general immune response, their loss impairs the total effectiveness of the immune system.

Once it has located a helper T cell, the virus binds to the cell's membrane and injects its genetic material. This viral genetic material releases enzymes that break open the host cell's genetic material, making it possible for the virus to insert its own information. The inserted material reprograms the helper T cell, causing it to stop performing its usual jobs for the immune system and become a factory that makes new HIV particles. Newly released viral material then travels to and invades other helper T cells. Production of a virus by the host cell does not destroy the cell immediately. Consequently, an invaded cell is able to make more of the virus for some time.

Importance of Helper T Cells

Without the helper T cells, some parts of the immune system cannot be called into action. These cells, which activate and coordinate other cells such as B lymphocytes, are clearly an important link in a chain of events that activates the immune system.

Early in an HIV infection, helper T cell count remains high enough for the immune system to function fairly well, even though the virus is present and has begun infecting cells. Eventually, so many helper T cells are infected and damaged that the victim's healthy helper T cell count drops dangerously, hampering the body's ability to fight infection. At this stage, the infected person is considered to have AIDS. On the average, it takes about ten years for HIV to destroy enough helper T cells to damage the immune system beyond repair.

Decline and Death

The immune systems of AIDS victims continue to collapse over time but HIV-infected persons do not die of AIDS specifically. Instead, death results from infections by viruses, bacteria, fungi, and other microbes that a healthy person's body is usually able to defeat. Such organisms are called opportunistic agents because under ordinary circumstances they would not be fatal. However, the immune system of an AIDS victim cannot launch a defense against them, so they reproduce and eventually overcome their host. Opportunistic infections in AIDS victims produce a variety of symptoms, including coughing, shortness of breath, seizures, difficulty swallowing, diarrhea, fever, vomiting, weight loss, fatigue, headaches, and coma.

AIDS victims are also prone to developing cancers, especially those brought on by other viruses. For example, many people with AIDS have Kaposi's sarcoma, a very rare cancer in which round dark spots develop on the skin and in the mouth. Cancers of the immune system, known as lymphomas, are also common in AIDS cases. In AIDS victims these and other cancers spread unusually fast and are very difficult to treat.

The Story Behind Survivors

A very small number of people infected with HIV, about 5 percent of all victims, never develop any symptoms. Scientists are interested in learning why these people stay healthy. One theory suggests that these people have immune systems with characteristics that protect them from the deadly virus. Another idea is that these 5 percent may have contracted a less aggressive strain of the virus.

A Unique Virus

Unlike other worldwide epidemics such as polio and measles, AIDS is still spreading. AIDS causes fear among many people, and with good reason. It is incurable and usually deadly. There is no vaccine against it, and it spreads quickly from one person to the next.

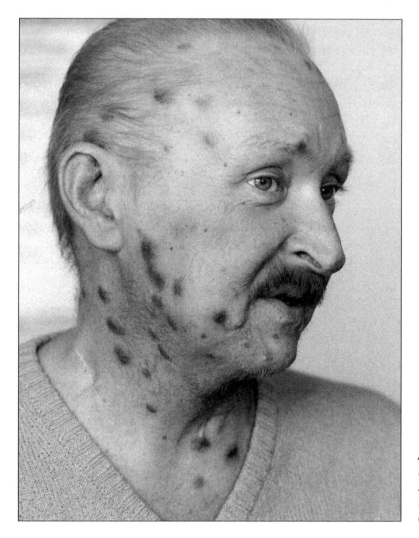

A rare cancer known as Kaposi's sarcoma causes round dark spots to develop on the skin.

AIDS is transmitted from an infected person to a noninfected person by exchange of blood or some other body fluid. AIDS victims in the early stages of infection may be completely unaware of their condition. During this time, an infected person potentially can share the virus with dozens of other people, who may continue its spread.

Unprotected sex is the most common way of transmitting AIDS. According to the Centers for Disease Control and Prevention (CDC), in the United States the chance of contracting HIV during an unprotected heterosexual encounter is one in one thousand. In some parts of the world, the risk is higher. During unprotected sex, the virus enters the body through the lining of the vagina, penis, or mouth. The chances of spreading this disease are significantly reduced when a man wears a condom during sex.

AIDS can also be transmitted in other ways. At one time, hospital patients were at risk of contracting HIV through blood transfusions. However, the CDC reports that screening techniques implemented in 1982 have insured that donated blood is safe. The virus also can be spread through shared use of intravenous needles. If an HIV victim injects drugs into his or her veins and does not discard or sterilize the needle, that needle becomes a lethal weapon. It harbors HIV and can transmit it to someone else who uses it or inadvertently handles it while working or playing in areas frequented by drug users. Fortunately, needles used in health care facilities pose little danger. It is rare for a health care worker to become infected with HIV from accidental sticks with contaminated needles.

If a pregnant woman is infected, the virus can travel across the placenta to her unborn baby. About one-fourth to one-third of women infected with HIV pass the virus to their babies. Babies also can get the virus from breast-feeding. If a mother is infected with HIV, the baby can acquire it through breast milk.

There is no cure for AIDS. Most treatments for its victims focus on slowing the spread of HIV particles in the body, treating opportunistic infections, and strengthening the immune system. Antiviral drugs show promise because they interfere with HIV's ability to replicate. Early in the AIDS epidemic, people infected with HIV were much sicker than many victims in the United States are today. At first, most Americans and Europeans with the disease spent a lot of time in the hospital, and many died within two years of infection. With current treatments, most infected people can remain healthy for decades.

What Not to Fear

HIV is a rather fragile virus that can be transmitted only in specific ways. It cannot be spread through the air or in the environment like a cold or flu virus. Lab tests by the CDC have shown that after blood, saliva, or sexual body fluids containing HIV have dried, the chance of transmission is nearly zero. Therefore, it cannot be transferred from one person to another on a toilet seat. Nor can it be transmitted by sharing a drinking glass or swimming in the pool with an infected person.

Although researchers have been able to detect low levels of HIV in the saliva of infected people, there is only a slight chance of transmission through kissing and biting. Saliva contains some antiviral properties that interfere with the virus's ability to infect others. Only one case of transmission by kissing has ever been documented by the CDC. There are no known cases of viral transmission through tears or sweat.

Research has also shown that AIDS cannot be spread by bloodsucking insects. Even in areas where the disease is prevalent and mosquito populations are high, HIV is not carried from one person to the next by insect bites. Mosquitoes bite people to take in blood, which is their food. When a mosquito bites a person, it injects its saliva into that person. However, it does not inject its blood or the blood of previous bite victims. If a mosquito bites an HIV positive person, it may take in a few viral particles. These viruses cannot replicate in mosquitoes. When mosquitoes feed, they do not travel from one person to the next, consuming as much blood as possible. Instead, they rest after each feeding so they can digest their blood meal. During this time, the virus dies.

Other Immunosuppressed Conditions

AIDS has gained a lot of attention in the world as a disease that suppresses the immune system. However, other conditions can have the same effect. Any type of immunodeficiency that does not appear until after birth is called an acquired immunodeficiency. The acquisition can be due to disease, as with AIDS in adults, or to injury or organ damage. For example, since the spleen helps trap and destroy infective organisms, problems with the spleen may lead to immune system challenges. Malnutrition can also slow down the immune system. However, when good nutrition is restored, the immune system generally recovers.

Some people suffer from immunodeficiency diseases at birth. These conditions are usually due to inherited, or genetic, disorders. There are several different immunodeficiency diseases, and they all affect different parts of the immune system. Some reduce levels of white blood cells. In other conditions, white blood cell levels are normal, but the cells are unable to function. In a few diseases, white blood cells function very well, but other components of the immune system are abnormal or missing.

Certain drugs and medical treatments can break down the body's natural defenses, permitting normally harmless organisms to cause dangerous infections. Treatments for cancer such as chemotherapy, radiation therapy, and immunosuppressive drugs interfere with normal immune function. An ideal cancer treatment would kill only cancerous tissues, but no such treatment exists. Chemicals, radiation, and medications that suppress the growth of cancer cells also kill normal body cells such as those in the immune system.

How to Stay Safe

People who have depressed or damaged immune systems are always advised to be extra careful to avoid exposure to disease-causing organisms. There are several steps that can

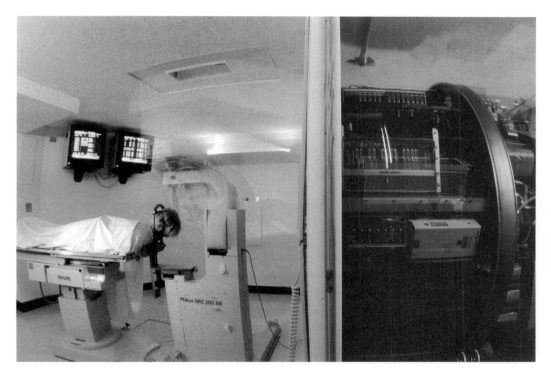

reduce risk of infection. Hand washing is the most effective way to prevent spread of disease from one person to another. A susceptible person also can be isolated in a room within the home or hospital. If visitors entering the room wear sterile gowns, gloves, and masks, any disease-causing organisms that may be present in or on their bodies will be prevented from spreading.

A patient undergoes radiation therapy to kill a brain tumor. Unfortunately, radiation also kills normal immune cells.

The Daily Battle

The human body has developed a complicated system for protecting itself. In a sense, the body is the site of daily battles in each person's lifelong war against microbes. When invaded, the body follows a well-choreographed plan in which it releases cells and chemicals to destroy invaders, cleans up debris, and prepares for future battles.

If the immune system is lacking one or more components, its ability to function is compromised and immunodeficiency disease results. People suffering from an immunodeficiency

Hand washing prevents the spread of disease from one person to another.

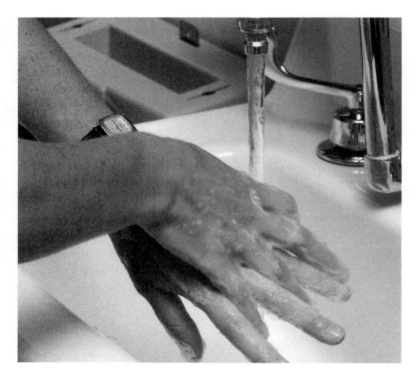

disorder are susceptible to a host of opportunistic diseases and are obliged to take extra precautions to protect themselves. Such disorders can be inherited, acquired through infection, or produced accidentally by drugs or other medical treatments. The human immunodeficiency virus, first identified in 1981, gave people around the globe a quick lesson in immune system appreciation. AIDS has clearly demonstrated for millions of people the value of an intact immune system.

3 | Allergies: False Alarms for the Immune System

Trillions of specialized cells work together to maintain good health in the human body. Cells of the immune system are designed to eliminate foreign substances that could damage the body. When these cells perform their jobs correctly, they play essential roles in maintaining good health. But if these cells make mistakes and respond to false alarms, they actually hurt the body instead of helping it.

Any harmless material that stimulates the immune system and causes it to attack is called an allergen. The response produced in the body to an allergen is an allergic or hypersensitive reaction. The intensity of such a reaction varies from person to person.

Not everyone experiences the same kinds of allergic reactions. A few people are sensitive to only one type of allergen. However, most people with allergies react to several normally harmless particles such as dust, molds, pollen, or animal dander. This is because all allergies develop from a common source: a hypersensitive immune system.

Scientists are not sure why some people have allergies and others do not, but they are reasonably certain that genetics plays a role. Studies show that if a child has one parent with allergies, that child has a 30 percent chance of developing them too. When both parents have allergies, the child stands a 50 percent chance of developing allergic reactions.

In the normally functioning immune system, B cells and other types of white blood cells travel freely through the body looking for antigens. However, in people with allergic reactions, the B cells malfunction, mistakenly identifying harmless particles as antigens. Then the B cells transform into plasma cells which produce antibodies against these wrongly identified particles or allergens.

Plasma cells can produce five different types of antibodies. During an allergic reaction, they only produce one of these types, the immunoglobulin E (IgE) antibody. Allergy sufferers have much higher levels of IgE in their blood than nonsufferers. Like other antibodies, IgE are specific to a particular allergen; one IgE reacts to cat dander, and a different one reacts to pollen. Scientists do not fully understand why the body even produces IgE since they serve no useful function. Some believe that at one time in human development, they may have played a role in protecting against parasitic worm infections. Whatever their functions in the past, IgE are manufactured now in response to allergens.

Cells That Malfunction: The Allergic Reaction

An allergic person has some B cells that cannot distinguish harmless particles from harmful ones. The problem most likely began in the individual's genetic code. It may lack some vital piece of information needed for correct interpretation. In other words, the B cells were probably wrongly encoded at the genetic level.

Incorrect genetic coding produces B cells that wrongly identify antigens, then target them with large amounts of IgE. After a B cell's first exposure to an allergen, the IgE that it generates attach themselves to two types of cells: mast cells and basophils. Basophils are found throughout the body, whereas mast cells are concentrated in the respiratory and gastrointestinal tracts as well as deep layers of the skin. The process in which IgE locate and bind to mast cells and basophils is called sensitization.

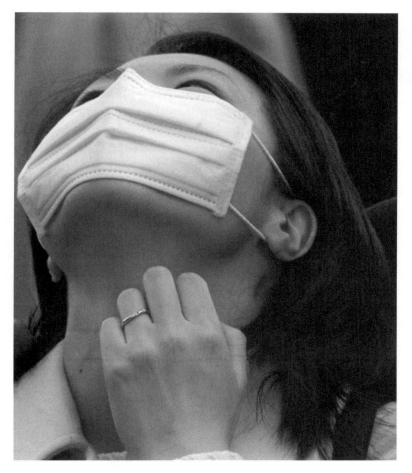

A woman wears a face mask for protection from allergens that cause hay fever.

Unwanted Histamines

Basophils and mast cells have a common trait; they both contain the chemical called histamine. Histamine normally plays an important role in fighting infection. But when it is released into the body at inappropriate times, or in excessive amounts, it can cause a variety of unpleasant symptoms such as wheezing, sneezing, itching, runny nose, swelling, and hives. About ten days after the first exposure of B cells to an allergen, mast cells and basophils are fully sensitized. After that, exposure of these cells to the offending allergen causes a release of histamine and the unpleasant symptoms of an allergic reaction. Over time, some people lose their sensitivity to specific allergens and no longer suffer.

On a cellular level, all allergic reactions have identical mechanisms. No matter what type of allergen is involved, the same sequence of events takes place in the bodies of allergic people. First, from their points of attachment on basophils and mast cells, IgE identify an allergen that enters the body. Next, the IgE attach to the surface of the allergen. The binding of the mast cells and basophils by way of the antibodies to the allergen initiates step three, release of complement proteins. These proteins travel to the site of the allergen and attach to it. Once attached, the complement proteins are able to destroy the mast cells and basophils, releasing their stores of histamine and other chemicals in the process. These chemicals then seep into the bloodstream where they have several effects. Histamine causes blood vessels to dilate, which enables them to hold more blood. The chemicals also open tiny spaces in the walls of blood vessels, allowing plasma to leak out into the tissues through these openings. Depending on the allergen and the part of the body involved in the allergic reaction, several symptoms can follow. If the mouth is the site of reaction, swelling and itching of the tongue may take place. Wheezing and breathing difficulties can occur if the allergic reaction takes place in the trachea and bronchi. Allergic reactions in the digestive tract produce stomach cramps, vomiting, and diarrhea. The skin responds to this cascade of events by forming rashes and the swollen bumps called hives.

Type I Allergic Reactions

Experts generally refer to allergies of the most common kinds as Type I. These are the sensitivities that people generally associate with the term "allergy." In a Type I reaction, response to the allergen occurs quickly. Once the body has been sensitized to an allergen, the immune system responds immediately to any reexposures. In a Type I reaction the release of chemicals by the mast cells and basophils produces inflammation. Almost any allergen (dust, pollen, drugs, or foods) can cause a Type I allergic reaction in sensitized people.

For some very sensitive people, a Type I allergic reaction can become life threatening. An extreme response to an allergen is described as anaphylaxis. Although almost any substance can cause an anaphylactic reaction in sensitive people, the common culprits are certain medications, foods, and insect stings. Anaphylactic shock, the terminal form of anaphylaxis, kills hundreds of people in the United States each year.

Severe Reactions and Identifying the Allergen

In an anaphylactic reaction, release of histamine and other chemicals causes severe inflammation and a sudden drop in blood pressure. Victims of anaphylaxis also have experienced heart palpitations, tingling, itching, flushed skin, throbbing ears, coughing, sneezing, difficulty breathing, and feelings of impending doom. In some cases, airways of the throat become dangerously constricted. Respiratory distress can result if immediate medical treatment is not provided. The alarming symptoms of anaphylaxis appear soon after exposure to the allergen, invariably within two hours.

Persons experiencing anaphylactic symptoms need to be transported to the closest emergency room. Those whose breathing is compromised are immediately treated with an injection of epinephrine, a hormone naturally produced by the adrenal glands, to widen the airways and strengthen the heartbeat. Without such treatment, death can occur in as little as three to four minutes after exposure to the allergen. Anyone who has experienced a severe allergic reaction is at risk of having another one and should consciously avoid that allergen in the future.

People who experience Type I allergic reactions sometimes visit a doctor called an allergist. The hardest part of the allergist's job may be identifying what allergen is causing the adverse reaction in the patient. To make a diagnosis, testing may be necessary. One of the most common methods used to identify allergies is a scratch test. Diluted

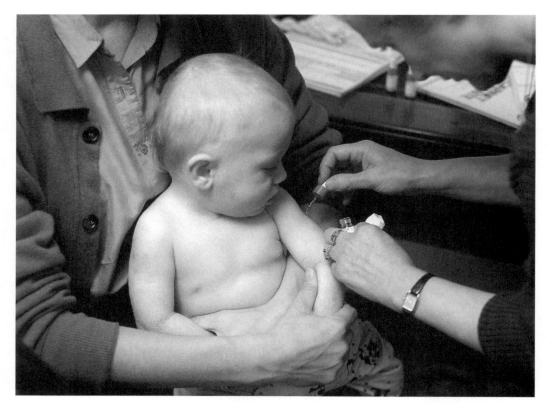

A baby gets an allergy scratch test to identify the allergen that has caused a severe skin rash.

extracts of several different allergens such as ragweed, cat dander, grass, molds, and tree pollen are applied to skin on the patient's back or arm. Each of these sites is then scratched with a needle. If a person is allergic, the site containing that extract will develop a wheal, or hivelike swelling, within twenty minutes. This wheal indicates that IgE to that allergen are present in the person's bloodstream. Some people test positive to more than one allergen.

For confirmation of an allergen, the doctor can also order radioallergosorbent (RAST) blood tests. These measure the levels of IgE to specific allergens in the blood. This blood test is particularly helpful in identifying offending allergens in seasonal allergic reactions, asthma reactions, and skin reactions. Neither the scratch test nor blood test is 100 percent accurate, but when their results are coupled with patient history, the allergist can usually arrive at a diagnosis and treatment plan.

Allergens Are Everywhere

Some allergies are seasonal. For example, hay fever occurs in the spring and fall when the pollen counts are high. Watery eyes, itchy throat, runny nose, and sneezing are common problems associated with hay fever. These symptoms are sometimes relieved by antihistamines, medications that block histamine production. Allergy sufferers can also reduce their symptoms by limiting the amount of time spent outdoors. Also, since pollen counts are lowest in the middle of the day, on cool days, and after it rains, it is helpful to stay inside at other times.

Allergens such as dust mites, feathers, animal dander, and mold may occur year round. These trigger a condition known as perennial allergic rhinitis. Nasal and ear congestion are also associated with perennial allergic rhinitis along with symptoms similar to those of hay fever. Sometimes congestion leads to sinus infections. Like seasonal allergies, perennial allergic rhinitis can be treated with antihistamines. Decongestants help to constrict blood vessels and shrink swollen nasal membranes, relieving nasal stuffiness.

Animal dander is just dry skin that household pets and other animals shed. When inhaled, dander causes an allergic response in some people. Cat dander can be a difficult problem for some individuals because when cats groom themselves, licking their coats, the dander spreads from their skin to their fur, where it is readily released into the air. Even though most cats are not fond of baths, a weekly wash reduces the amount of dander on a cat.

In dust allergies, the allergen producing the symptoms is not usually the dust itself, but a tiny organism called a dust mite. These mites live in carpets, upholstery, and pillows. To reduce dust mites in a home, bedding should be washed frequently. Specialists sometimes recommend replacing drapes with blinds, and carpets with wood or vinyl floors, as good ways to keep the house free of dust. Allergies to molds are caused by mold spores. Since molds grow in dark, damp places, a person who is allergic to mold spores should avoid

areas like basements. The use of anti-mildew sprays in damp parts of the house can also help.

Food and Drug Allergies

Some foods can also cause allergic reactions. About 1 percent of the U.S. population suffers from food allergies. Peanuts and shellfish are two foods that cause problems. Food additives and other chemicals in food can also cause allergies. The first indication of a food allergy is typically a skin rash accompanied by disturbances of the gastrointestinal tract. Some raw fruits and vegetables like strawberries and tomatoes can also cause itching around the mouth and lips in susceptible persons. Cooking these foods helps eliminate the allergic reaction because it changes the protein structure of the allergen.

Extreme reactions to foods can cause hives, asthma, and anaphylaxis. Diagnosis of food allergies often has to be determined by an elimination diet. During this process all foods that are potential allergens are eliminated from the diet, then reintroduced one at a time to determine which one triggers the allergic reaction.

Certain drugs can act as allergens in some people, and after a single exposure to a specific drug, reexposure to that same drug at a later date may produce an allergic response in a sensitive person. Rashes, hives, or anaphylaxis are possible consequences of such reexposure. The most common drug allergies are to penicillin and sulfa drugs. At one time, these drugs were the only medications available to treat bacterial infections, so they were given to a lot of patients. Some of the recipients developed allergies to them.

Drug allergies can affect specific organs. Drugs used to treat high blood pressure or high cholesterol may lead to hypersensitivity in the form of hepatitis, or inflammation of the liver. Having allergic reactions to drugs is not the same as experiencing unpleasant effects of medications. So-called side effects have nothing to do with the immune system. Swelling and hives from a penicillin shot are allergic reactions to the penicillin. A stomachache from taking penicillin capsules is a side effect. Medications that cause allergic reactions should be avoided, whereas adverse side effects often can be tolerated.

Allergy Shots

In any type of allergy, the best treatment is precaution: avoidance of all allergens. Unfortunately, in some cases the allergen cannot be escaped. It is impossible to completely eliminate allergens like pollen and mold from life. In many cases immunotherapy can help. During immunotherapy, a patient receives a series of injections of the offending allergen. A very weak dilution is used at the beginning of the treatment. The concentration of allergen is slowly increased over time. Injections of allergens stimulate production of antibodies that block the IgE molecules, preventing them from interacting with the allergens. As a result, histamine is not released and allergy symptoms are avoided. The success rate of immunotherapy is generally good. After three to five years the shots usually can be stopped. Immunotherapy does not work for everyone, however. It is usually the most effective with pollen, dust mites, insect venom, and animal dander. There is some risk with immunotherapy because a few people react adversely to these injections. For this reason patients are asked to remain in the doctor's office for twenty minutes following each injection to see if itching, sneezing, coughing, wheezing, and hives may occur. If these symptoms show up in the patient, antihistamines or epinephrine may be needed to stop the allergic reaction.

Incompatible Blood Types

Any type of nonself molecule can act as an antigen and stimulate the immune system to release antibodies. Thus a physician giving a blood transfusion to a patient is transferring cells from one person into the circulatory system of another person, and these nonself cells can trigger an allergic reaction. Transfusions often are necessary, however, to replace blood that has been lost, to improve the blood's ability to carry oxygen, or to promote clotting. When a donor's blood cells are transfused into a recipient, the recipient's immune system examines the cells to determine if they are self or nonself. If the surface markers of donor's and recipient's red blood cells are the same, the donated blood is viewed as self, and the donated blood is compatible with the recipient's blood. However, donor blood cells are perceived as nonself if their surface markers differ from those of the recipient's blood cells, and in such cases the two bloods are incompatible.

Transfusion of incompatible blood triggers a Type II immune response in the recipient. Antibodies in the recipient's blood bind to incompatible donated blood cells, causing them to clump and to rupture. This cellular damage triggers mast cells to release histamine. Because histamine dilates

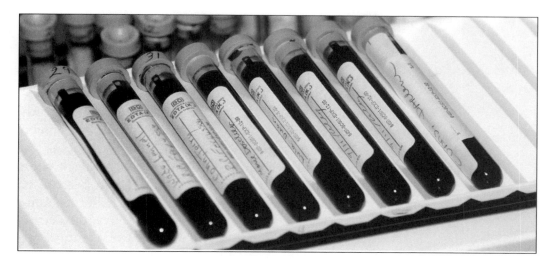

blood vessels, blood is suddenly traveling through a larger space, so blood pressure drops. Histamine also affects the walls of blood vessels, making them leaky. Fluid oozes out of the leaky vessels, reducing blood volume and further lowering blood pressure. When blood pressure is low, the amount of blood flowing into and out of the heart with each heartbeat is low. As a result the recipient experiences difficulty breathing, anxiety, intense headache, and neck and chest pain. In severe reactions the recipient can die.

Thankfully, transfusions generally occur in hospitals where they are closely monitored. To minimize chances of reaction, several precautions are taken. After double-checking that donor and recipient blood are compatible types, the transfusion is begun and the recipient is closely observed to allow a rapid response if problems arise.

Blood for transfusions must match the recipient's blood type. A transfusion of incompatible blood can cause death.

Type III and IV Reactions

When the body mistakenly identifies some of its own cells as foreign, doctors say that a Type III allergic reaction has occurred. In such cases the immune system makes antibodies against part of its own body. Antibodies coat these targeted body cells, forming large immune complexes. As a result, the normally functioning body cells are attacked and damaged by complement proteins. Type III reactions lead to a variety of disorders known as autoimmune diseases.

Delayed allergic reactions that occur twelve to seventy-two hours after exposure to an allergen are identified as Type IV. An example of a Type IV reaction is the inflammatory response caused by poison ivy and poison oak. Allergic reactions to these plants do not occur upon contact, but a day or two after exposure. Another example is the skin antigen challenge test for tuberculosis. When a person is tested to see if they have been exposed to tuberculosis, their skin is injected with a small amount of serum containing disabled tuberculosis-causing bacteria. If the person has ever had TB, their skin will swell at the injection site within forty-eight to seventy-eight hours.

Final Take on Allergies

Sneezing and sniffling are not necessarily symptoms of colds. The immune system sometimes overreacts to common everyday substances. The goal of this watchdog system is to prevent invading microbes from entering the body. When sensitive cells become confused and mistake harmless particles for serious invaders, the symptoms of an allergic reaction appear.

The term "allergy" comes from the Greek word *allos*, or "other," indicating a change from the original state. An allergy is an altered or changed response of the immune system to a normally harmless substance. Allergies can develop at any age and they affect the health of millions each year. People can be allergic to a variety of substances including pollen, animal venoms, dust mites, and food. Most allergic reactions simply cause irritating symptoms such as itching, runny nose, swelling, or watery eyes. However, some reactions are life threatening and require immediate medical attention.

For years people have looked for solutions to their allergies. Today there are some treatments available. Antihistamines and decongestants are effective for most people. For long-term relief immunotherapy, or allergy shots, helps the body develop a mechanism to stop the allergic sequence of events.

4 Autoimmune Diseases: When the Body Attacks Itself

The network of cells and organs that make up the immune system works to protect the body from invaders. When the system gets confused and mistakes harmless substances for dangerous ones, consequences can be uncomfortable, as in mild allergic reactions. However, if the immune system's recognition procedure breaks down and it is unable to distinguish self and nonself cells, disease can result.

The prefix "auto" means self. In autoimmune diseases, the immune system mistakenly attacks itself, zeroing in on the cells, tissues, and organs of its own body, destroying the very cells it was meant to protect. These attacks on self produce inflammation and damage. There are many different types of autoimmune diseases that can attack one tissue, one organ, or several tissues and organs throughout the body.

Normally, white blood cells produce antibodies against foreign cells they encounter as they travel through the body. In autoimmune diseases, white blood cells mistakenly make antibodies against the body's own cells. Antibodies produced against self are called autoantibodies. In a healthy immune system the white blood cells do not act against self cells. Most autoimmune diseases stem from the manufacture of abnormal T cells, which stimulate production of the misguided autoantibodies. When these autoantibodies attack self tissues, the tissues are damaged.

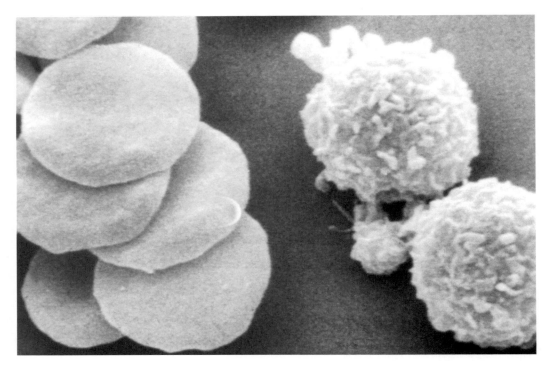

White blood cells (right) are different in shape and function from the flat, saucer-like red blood cells (left).

The "Why" Behind Autoimmune Diseases

The causes of autoimmune diseases are not well understood, but scientists believe that several factors are involved. Genetics definitely plays a role. Several genes, which may be carried by up to 20 percent of the population, are believed to increase a person's chance of developing autoimmune diseases. The presence of these genes does not mean that a person will definitely suffer an autoimmune disease, but it does constitute a predisposition; that is, it raises the odds. It is clearly established that relatives of people with autoimmune diseases are more likely than the general population to develop autommimmune diseases themselves.

It takes more than genes for a person to get sick with an autoimmune disease. Someone with these predisposing genes also must be exposed to an outside agent that activates them. Outside agents are called environmental triggers, and they vary with the disease. The autoimmune disease rheumatoid fever follows an infection with bacteria of the genus *Streptococcus*. Sunlight can be enough to precipitate a case of lupus, a different autoimmune condition. Ingestion of dietary iodine can trigger autoimmune diseases of the thyroid gland. Aging, stress, hormones, or pregnancy can cause other autoimmune diseases.

Scientists are trying to identify the environmental conditions that trigger each different autoimmune disease. If susceptible people know the triggers, they can avoid them. Statistics show that approximately 50 million Americans suffer from some type of autoimmune disease. Of this figure about 30 million are women of childbearing age, leading scientists to investigate further the role of female hormones in autoimmune diseases.

Organ Specificity in Autoimmune Diseases

Autoimmune diseases are usually classified into one of two broad groups: organ specific or non–organ specific. In organ-specific disorders, the immune system targets one organ. Non–organ-specific disorders are the autoimmune diseases that attack various parts of the body at once.

Autoimmune diseases of both groups affect the body in a number of ways. They can destroy specific cells and tissues, stimulate organs to grow larger than normal, or cause organs to malfunction. Some areas of the body that are common targets for autoimmune diseases include the pancreas, thyroid gland, adrenal gland, red blood cells, connective tissue, skin, muscles, and joints. It is possible to have more than one autoimmune disorder at the same time.

Lupus: The Butterfly Rash Disease

Systemic lupus erythematosus (SLE) is a non–organ-specific disease that causes a variety of symptoms. People with lupus can be affected in the joints, skin, kidneys, heart, lungs, blood vessels, and the brain. Because it can damage tissues in almost any part of the body, lupus is described as a nonorgan disease. The symptoms vary extremely, from

Lupus can cause a butterfly-shaped rash across the nose and cheeks.

mild to severe. Women between the ages of fifteen and forty-five are the group most likely to develop SLE. It is also more prevalent in African American, Hispanic, Native American, and Asian women than in Caucasian women. Some common problems associated with lupus include extreme fatigue, painful and swollen joints, unexplained fevers, skin rashes, and kidney disorders. Some people also experience chest pain, hair loss, anemia, pale-colored fingers, headaches, and depression. Many people with lupus develop a butterfly-shaped rash across the nose and the cheeks.

Diagnosis of lupus can be difficult. A complete medical history and an array of laboratory tests are needed to identify this disease. No single lab test can indicate lupus, but several together provide clues that help doctors piece the puzzle together. One very useful blood assessment is an antinuclear antibody test (ANA). In this procedure, laboratory technicians examine a blood sample for the presence of autoantibodies that react against the nuclei of the patient's own cells. In lupus patients, B cells make antibodies that will react with self cell nuclei. The resulting antigen-antibody complexes can be detected in the ANA test. A positive result does not confirm lupus, because other immune disorders can also cause positive results. But it does provide useful information.

To confirm the diagnosis, doctors also order other blood work, including an erythrocyte sedimentation rate (ESR). The ESR measures how long it takes red blood cells to settle to the bottom of the test tube. When inflammation is present in the body, sedimentation rates are higher than normal.

Effective treatments for lupus vary from one patient to the next. Sometimes antimalarial drugs are used to treat fatigue and joint inflammation. Patients whose worst symptom is joint pain are often prescribed nonsteroidal anti-inflammatory drugs (NSAIDs) or over-the-counter medications like Motrin, Advil, Naprosyn, or Aleve. However, the most common drugs used for stiff joints are corticosteroid hormones. These are synthetic anti-inflammatory hormones. Some nasty side effects can result from their long-term use.

Physicians are careful to instruct lupus patients about their disease because they need to understand it to manage it. Avoiding exposure to the sun is important because sunlight may worsen the disease. Many doctors suggest that women with lupus refrain from taking birth control pills or using hormone replacement therapy because additional estrogen may worsen symptoms.

Rheumatoid Arthritis: A Disease of Joint Destruction

The systemic autoimmune disorder called rheumatoid arthritis (RA) usually targets the tissues that line joints, causing severe swelling, pain, and stiffness. Inflammation of the joint

Women are more likely than men to be affected by rheumatoid arthritis.

lining sets off fluid leakage into the joint, producing yet more swelling. Inflammation usually occurs in the joints on both sides of the body at the same time. The wrists, fingers, knees, feet, and ankles are commonly affected. Over time, cartilage that normally separates the joints begins to wear out and is replaced by hard deposits of the mineral calcium. The underlying bone is eventually affected. Deformities can result from cartilage destruction, bone erosion, and tendon inflammation. Some people develop hard, painless nodules under the skin near the elbow or Achilles tendon. Some other common symptoms of RA are fatigue, malaise, loss of appetite, morning stiffness, and swollen glands.

Even though RA is most common in joints, it can also affect some organs. If the disease damages bone marrow, it can cause reduction in red blood cell production. This may result in anemia. The heart, lungs, blood vessels, and eyes can also be targets of this autoimmune disease.

As in lupus, genetics, hormones, and infectious agents are thought to play a role in the development of rheumatoid arthritis. Women are two-and-a-half times as likely to be affected as men. RA is believed to occur in as much as 1 to 2 percent of the population, making it the most common autoimmune disease.

Onset of RA usually occurs between the ages of twenty-five and fifty-five. The severity of the disease varies from person to person.

Diagnosis of rheumatoid arthritis is difficult. Laboratory tests and a thorough medical history help determine if a person has RA. Results from ESR tests usually show that sedimentation rates are elevated. Hemoglobin levels in the blood may be below normal. In about 75 percent of people with RA a component called rheumatoid factor is found in the blood. Other tests that may be helpful include X rays of the joints and a laboratory analysis of the fluid around the joints to assess the amount of damage at these sites.

Most people with rheumatoid arthritis require lifelong treatment plans, since there is no cure for the disease. These plans include medications, physical therapy, and sometimes surgery to reduce pain. Doctors know that early and aggressive treatment of RA delays joint deterioration. People with RA can reduce pain by performing daily range of motion exercises, using hot and cold treatments on joints, taking frequent rest periods between activities, and getting eight to ten hours of sleep each night.

Over-the-counter NSAIDs like Motrin, Advil, and Naprosyn are commonly used to reduce inflammation and pain, as well as prescription medications such as Vioxx and Celebrex. When anti-inflammatory and pain medications do not provide adequate relief, doctors may suggest disease-modifying antirheumatic drugs (DMARDs) such as gold compounds and antimalarial medications. Some toxic side effects have been noted in the DMARDs, so their use requires continuous supervision by the physician. Corticosteroids are also used to reduce inflammation when other therapies fail. One promising medication for RA is called Enbrel. This drug acts by interfering with the activity of an inflammatory protein. Drugs to suppress the immune system are the last line of defense for RA patients because it is preferable to avoid the life-threatening complications that develop when the entire immune system is shut down.

The progression of the disease varies among individuals. Many people respond favorably to treatments and live normal lives. Some people go into remission, periods when symptoms go away, in the first year of the disease. If a patient does not experience remission within fifteen years of onset, there is only a 20 percent chance it will ever occur. Even so, most people who develop rheumatoid arthritis are physically able to maintain full-time employment. Only about 10 percent of rheumatoid arthritis patients are so severely disabled that they cannot perform daily activities of caring for themselves.

Multiple Sclerosis: Still a Mystery to Scientists

Multiple sclerosis (MS), unlike rheumatoid arthritis and lupus, targets specific organ systems. In MS, the immune system affects the tissues of the central nervous system. Even though multiple sclerosis has been studied for a long time, many factors concerning it still remain a mystery for scientists.

Like many other autoimmune diseases, the symptoms of MS can be mild or severe. In multiple sclerosis the body's immune system attacks and damages the myelin sheath that surrounds the nerves of the brain and spinal cord. The function of a myelin sheath is to help conduct nerve signals. If it is damaged, signals cannot travel quickly along the nerves, and the systems served by those nerves are impaired. Symptoms of MS include tingling and burning sensations from impairment of sensory nerve transmissions and weakness or paralysis from impairment of motor control signals. Other problems caused by MS are inability to perform smooth motions, fatigue, bowel and bladder problems, lack of coordination, and visual disturbances.

Multiple sclerosis is found in approximately three out of one thousand people. Children of parents with MS are ten times more likely to develop it than the general population. Most people experience initial symptoms of MS between the ages of twenty and forty, although it may not be diagnosed until years later. Caucasians are twice as likely as other races, and women are twice as likely as men, to develop the disease. Scientific research suggests that genetics plays a role in MS since groups such as Gypsies and Eskimos never get it. Experts also have evidence that it is triggered by an environmental factor such as a virus. One interesting fact about MS is that it is five times more common in temperate climates than in tropical regions. Canada and Scotland have high rates of MS while Africa and Asia have low rates.

Diagnosis of MS can be very frustrating for physicians. A history of symptoms over a long course of time and a diagnostic test, magnetic resonance imaging (MRI) of the brain, are helpful. MRI produces a three-dimensional image that

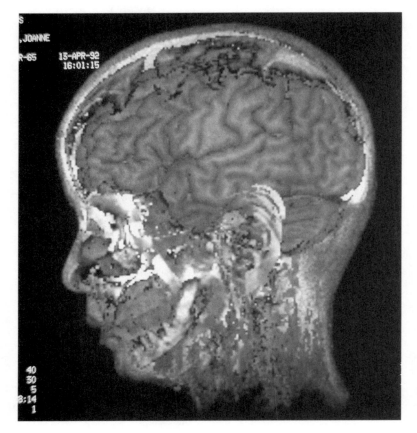

Magnetic resonance imaging (MRI) produces three-dimensional images of the brain.

can reveal patches of inflammation called plaques in the white matter of the brain. Plaques appear following the destruction of myelin in the nerves of the brain. The presence of these plaques on an MRI indicates myelin damage.

Another way to detect MS is through a lumbar puncture. In this test a needle is inserted in the spinal column and some spinal fluid is removed for analysis to determine antibody levels. High levels of antibodies are symptomatic of MS because the overactive immune system makes antibodies in huge amounts in response to the constant destruction of myelin. The nerve conduction test, yet another diagnostic tool, measures the time it takes for a nerve impulse generated by a specific stimulus to reach the brain. A reduced velocity may indicate that nerves have lost myelin, the substance that assists in conduction of nerve signals.

There is no known cure for multiple sclerosis, but for some people there are effective plans to manage the disease, at least early on. Treatment includes medications, healthy diets, physical therapy, and plenty of rest. MS patients should avoid heat. In most MS patients symptoms worsen when they are near hot objects or when their internal body temperature rises during exercise. Removal of the heat source or immersion in a cool bath can stop the cascade of symptoms.

Myasthenia Gravis: The Weak-Muscle Disease

The Latin words *myasthenia gravis* mean "gravely debilitated muscles." This autoimmune disease affects the nervous system: The immune system makes antibodies that interfere with the normal transmission of nerve signals to the muscles. Since the muscles do not get signals from the nerves, they fail to move properly.

The exact mechanism of nerve transmission that is damaged in myasthenia gravis involves the chemical called acetylcholine. Normally, when a nerve impulse reaches the place where the nerve attaches to a muscle, acetylcholine is released. This chemical flows from the nerve to the muscle, and binds to receptors on the muscle. Once it is bound in place, it causes the muscle to contract. In patients with myasthenia gravis, the immune system attacks and destroys many of the acetylcholine receptors on the muscle. Therefore, little of this neurotransmitter binds to the muscle, and the muscle does not contract properly. Sufferers of this disease complain of specific muscle weakness such as drooping eyelids, difficulty chewing or talking, or leg weakness. These symptoms worsen as the day progresses.

Like all autoimmune diseases myasthenia gravis is believed to have a genetic link. Statistics estimate fourteen out of every one hundred thousand Americans have this disease. Women usually develop it in their twenties and thirties while men develop it after age fifty. Diagnosis is based on patient history and laboratory testing. The most specific lab test checks the blood for the presence of antibodies to acetylcholine receptors on muscle tissue. These antibodies are present in 85 percent of patients. Because acetylcholine is blocked from its binding sites, drugs that increase the amount of acetylcholine improve muscle strength. A test using one of these drugs can confirm a positive diagnosis.

In most people with myasthenia gravis the face muscles are affected first, making it difficult to speak and swallow. Periods of fatigue with muscle weakness in the arms and legs are characteristic symptoms. The degree of muscle weakness can vary widely from day to day with severe phases followed by a return to almost normal function. In the worst cases people may become almost totally paralyzed, yet they never lose the feeling in their muscles. A few suffer such muscle weakness in their lungs that they need help breathing.

One of the treatments for this disease is administration of drugs that increase levels of acetylcholine. Corticosteroids and other medications that suppress production of antibodies may also be beneficial, although these drugs can only be used in limited amounts because they can cause dangerous side effects. Sometimes patients are helped by a plasma exchange which removes abnormal antibodies from their blood.

Psoriasis: Immune Assault on the Skin

Another organ-specific autoimmune disease is psoriasis. This skin condition is characterized by redness, itching, thick or dry skin, and silvery scales on the skin. Psoriasis may affect small areas of skin or it may cover the entire body with red scaly structures that vary in size and shape and can be quite painful. The trunk, elbows, knees, scalp, skin folds, or fingernails are normally the most common

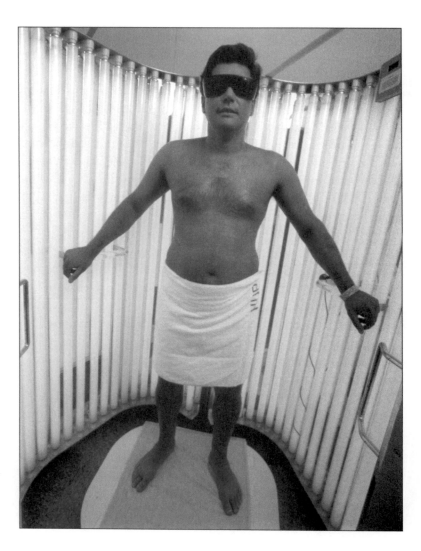

A psoriasis patient undergoes photo-therapy, a direct exposure to synthetic sunlight.

areas affected. Some people also experience joint aches. Psoriasis appears in eight out of every ten thousand Americans. It commonly occurs between the ages of fifteen and thirty-five years and is the most frequent in Caucasians. The outbreaks tend to come and go throughout the course of the disease.

Diagnosis is based on the characteristic scaling pattern of psoriasis. To confirm the diagnosis, some of the affected skin can be removed and examined under the microscope. Depending on the severity of the disease, medications usually treat psoriasis quite effectively. Antidandruff shampoos, antifungal medications, antibiotics, and cortisone creams help reduce symptoms when applied to the skin. In severe cases immunosuppressive medications are given. Phototherapy, or exposure to moderate light, alleviates symptoms in some people. To help control the disease patients should avoid bright sunlight, stressful situations, cold climates, cuts and rashes, and exposure to infectious agents.

Diabetes Mellitus: Blood Sugar Disorder

An autoimmune disease that can be especially devastating is diabetes mellitus. There are two forms of diabetes: type one is insulin dependent, and type two is noninsulin dependent. Only type one is an autoimmune disease. Type one is also called juvenile diabetes because it is normally present in children and adolescents. Of the two types of diabetes, type one accounts for only 5 to 10 percent of all cases.

The causes of type one diabetes are not known for certain, but experts think that environmental as well as genetic factors play roles, since appearance of this disease often follows a viral attack on the body. Type one diabetes targets and destroys insulin-producing cells of the pancreas. Insulin is a hormone that helps glucose gain entry into cells. Without enough insulin, glucose builds up in the blood of diabetics because it is not transported into body cells, which need it to provide energy. Excess glucose in the blood spills over into the excretory system and leaves the body through the kidneys and bladder. The process of ridding the body of excess glucose requires lots of water, so diabetics find themselves constantly thirsty.

Symptoms of diabetes include frequent urination, excessive thirst, unexplained weight loss, extreme hunger, sudden changes in vision, tingling and numbness in extremities, fatigue, sores that are slow to heal, dry skin, and a pronounced tendency to develop infections. Complications that can arise from this disease are increased risk of cardiovascular disease, stroke, and kidney failure. Many diabetics develop high blood pressure. Diabetes is the leading cause of new cases of blindness in adults. More than 50 percent of lower limb amputations in the United States occurs due to diabetes, and disease of the gums is 30 percent more prevalent in diabetes patients.

Diagnosis of diabetes is not nearly as complicated as diagnosis of some other autoimmune diseases. It simply requires a blood sample that can be tested for levels of glucose. A very specific blood test called a fasting glucose reveals a patient's blood level of glucose after a period of fasting. Urine can also be tested for glucose. A high level of glucose in urine indicates that the level also is high in the blood.

People with diabetes must keep their blood sugar levels low. Type one diabetics have to take insulin to replace that which is missing in their body. Insulin can be administered by an injection one or more times each day, or by a pump that delivers a small amount of insulin all through the day.

The Big Picture

Early in life, cells in the immune system acquire the ability to distinguish between self and nonself. Unless these cells can correctly identify nonself molecules when they encounter them, they cannot defend the body. These microscopic defenders must be able to distinguish cells that belong to the body from those that do not so they can identify, hunt down, and destroy invaders.

Unfortunately, the immune system does not always function properly. It can mistake normal body cells for nonself cells. Since its job is to destroy nonself cells, it attacks the

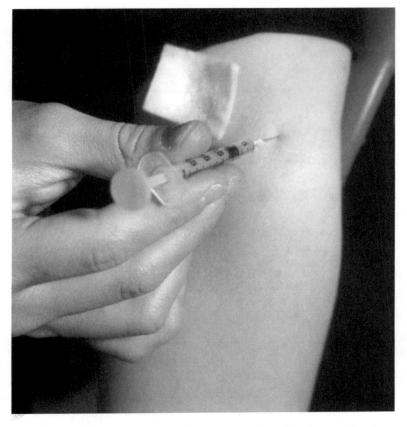

People with diabetes must inject themselves with insulin to keep their blood sugar levels low.

misidentified body cells with vigor and enthusiasm. During the attack, cells are damaged and the body suffers from an autoimmune disease.

The type of attack the body launches on its own tissues depends on which cells it has misidentified as nonself. In some cases, such as diabetes, rheumatoid arthritis, multiple sclerosis, and psoriasis, the body identifies only one organ as nonself. On the other hand, the body may attack several tissues or organs at once, as it does in lupus. In either case, victims of these conditions face a lifetime of disease management.

5 Using Medical Technologies

Throughout recorded history doctors have been working with their patients in the battle against disease. In the past, physicians have enjoyed little success because they lacked a clear understanding of the agents that cause diseases. However, work by early scientists laid the foundation for current studies on microbes and how they cause infections.

Today medical experts understand much more about how the immune system fights disease. Scientists are currently researching new technologies that can help strengthen and support the immune system. Some of these techniques are designed to trick the immune system, while other methods work to tame it.

Vaccines and Their History

Early in the twentieth century millions of people the world over died from infectious diseases. For example, in 1920 more than 21,000 cases of smallpox, 460,000 cases of measles, and 147,000 cases of diphtheria were reported in the United States. The number of fatalities exceeded 21,000. At that time very few treatments existed to prevent infections.

Since then, vaccines have been employed against these diseases and many others. The vaccine is one of the most powerful tools ever developed in the field of health. Scientists had their first glimpse at the potential of vaccines more than two hundred years ago. In 1796 an English physician named Edward Jenner made a vaccine to protect humans against the deadly smallpox virus. His work went unnoticed by most people. Yet it paved the way for future vaccines that are directly responsible for sparing millions of lives.

A vaccination, or immunization, mobilizes the body's natural defenses against an infectious disease. It provides immunity from a disease–causing organism before that organism can cause sickness. There is not a vaccine for every infectious disease in the world. However, since the mid–1900s, the United States has approved and licensed more than thirty vaccines. Many of these are given to the entire population. Nearly all American children are regularly immunized against measles, mumps, rubella (German measles), diphtheria, tetanus, whooping cough (pertussis), infection from the bacterium *Haemophilus influenzae* type B, hepatitis B, varicella (chicken pox), hepatitis A, pneumococcal disease, and polio.

Dr. Edward Jenner performs his first vaccination in 1796.

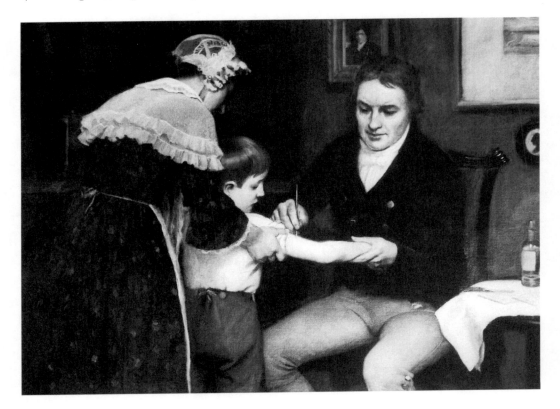

How Vaccines Work

Vaccines trick the immune system. They take advantage of the body's ability to develop immunity to a disease to which it has been exposed. In the disease process, germs invade and reproduce within the body. The immune system responds by making millions of antibody-producing white blood cells. In the natural world, by the time enough antibodies have been made to fight an infection, the person has already developed symptoms of the disease. After the body has overcome these invading germs, however, some antibodies remain in the blood to guard against future infections. If germs of the same kinds reappear, even many years later, the antibodies spring into action to kill them before illness can occur. In other words, the body is immune to reinfection by that same germ.

Vaccinations enable people to develop protection against a disease without ever catching that disease. They give the body a type of defense called acquired active immunity. Vaccines are made from modified disease-causing germs. The germs have been chemically weakened (attenuated) or even killed so that they cannot make the patient sick. However, they have enough of their cell surface markers intact to stimulate the immune system to make antibodies. A vaccine can be administered by mouth, nose, or injection. Once it is delivered into the body, the immune system reacts by producing antibodies, just as it would in response to the disease germ itself. These antibodies give the vaccinated individual decades of immunity to that disease.

Getting a Vaccination

Even though vaccinations are very safe, they are not perfect. Like other types of medicine, vaccinations do not work for 100 percent of the population. Some people do not respond to vaccines by developing immunity. A few people even have adverse reactions to vaccinations. These adverse reactions can be as mild as swelling at the site of injection or development of a low-grade fever. On rare occasions life-threatening anaphylactic reactions occur. Nevertheless, statisticians have determined that the risks of not getting vaccinated far outweigh the small risks of adverse reactions.

Most people get vaccinated when they are children. By the time babies are a few months old, they have lost the majority of the natural immunity acquired from their mothers' antibodies. Thus at six to eight weeks, babies in the United States start receiving vaccinations against diseases that can be fatal to children. Each disease has a separate vaccine. Several vaccines can be combined and given at one time without destroying the effectiveness of the other vaccines. Most vaccines are administered as injections. The DTP (made up of vaccines for diphtheria, tetanus, and pertussis) and MMR (which contains vaccines for measles, mumps, and rubella) are examples of some injections given to children.

The importance of vaccinations in infants and children cannot be overemphasized. The germs that caused deadly childhood illnesses in the early 1900s are still present in the environment and capable of producing the disease. In the 1940s and 1950s there were no vaccines for measles or polio. During those two decades thousands of children died of measles, and tens of thousands of children were crippled or killed by polio. In addition to protecting individual children, immunization safeguards entire communities against an outbreak of an epidemic disease that could make many unvaccinated children sick at the same time.

Before a new vaccine is released for public use, it must go through a stringent testing procedure by the Food and Drug Administration (FDA). First computer studies are used to predict what interaction each experimental vaccine will have with the immune system. Afterward, the new vaccines are tested on animals such as mice, guinea pigs, and monkeys. Finally, human volunteers are used in the testing process. Before a vaccine can be considered for public use it must be tried out on three groups of people. This process usually takes ten years or more to conclude. Even after the vaccine is made available to the public, it is kept under close scrutiny for several years.

The first American children were injected with the polio vaccine in 1954.

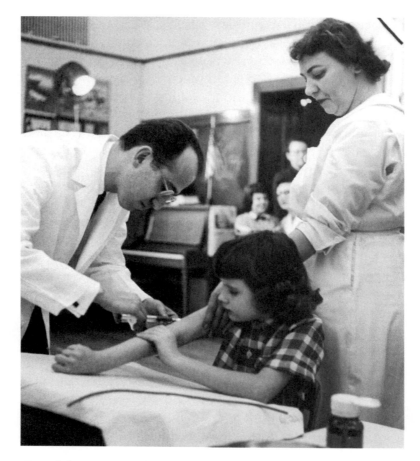

Problems with Making Vaccines

Vaccines have not been made against all infectious diseases. There are several reasons for this. For one thing, vaccines are not easy to manufacture. To make a safe and effective vaccine scientists must understand the nature of the target germ, how it enters the body, and how it spreads, as well as understand the human immune response to it. Moreover, some germs mutate, or change, over time. In nature mutations play an important role in providing variations in an organism. However, in medicine, mutations can cause problems because each strain or variation of a microbe requires a different vaccine. For instance, the virus that causes the common cold has many different strains. A person who catches several colds in a few months probably has been infected with several different strains of that virus. Since symptoms of the common cold are usually mild, scientists do not try to produce vaccines for each strain. However, every year scientists do try to predict which strain of influenza will be most likely to infect an area of the country. This is because influenza can be fatal to the elderly and persons with weakened immune systems. After scientists decide on the most likely strain, they develop a vaccination to that one strain and offer it to the sick or elderly. If the scientists make a mistake in predicting which strain will be most common, then the vaccination they create will protect only a relatively small number of people receiving the flu vaccine that year.

Gamma Globulins: Ready-Made Antibodies

Vaccines do not work overnight. After a vaccination it takes the body several weeks to produce antibodies. That is why the vaccine for the flu is best taken well before the start of the flu season. People who are exposed to a dangerous disease for which they have been vaccinated recently, or not at all, do not have time to develop active immunity to prevent them from getting sick. Such persons may be injected with ready-made antibodies to a disease. These antibodies, called gamma globulins, are taken from the bloodstream of a person who has already developed immunity to the disease. These ready-made antibodies immediately provide support for the recipient's immune system by giving an acquired passive immunity to the disease. The term "passive" indicates that the recipient's immune system did not manufacture the antibodies itself.

A good example of a disease that is treated by injections of gamma globulins is rabies, which is caused by a virus transmitted by the bite of an infected animal. The alarming symptoms of rabies may begin with paralysis in the legs and a feverish, agitated feeling. Within hours, the disease causes copious production of saliva and painful spasms in the throat.

The throat becomes so irritated that even a sip of water can cause it to spasm, hence the common name for rabies, "hydrophobia" (fear of water). The rabies virus works its way through the victim's nervous system until it reaches the brain, where it produces swelling. Asphyxia due to swollen airways, convulsions, and paralysis can result in death unless patients receive early medical intervention.

The general population is rarely vaccinated against rabies because their risk of developing the disease is low. Only people who work with animals all the time need the vaccination. However, if unvaccinated people are bitten by a rabid animal, their lives are in danger. Bite victims must receive five injections of rabies gamma globulins to fight the viral infection before the horrible symptoms of rabies appear.

Antibody injections such as the rabies gamma globulins offer protection only for a few weeks. If there is any danger of reexposure to the disease, the bite victim is generally advised to receive a vaccination. This will create active immunity and guarantee lifetime resistance to the disease.

Antitoxin Treatment

Antitoxin treatment is required to combat toxins, or poisons, produced by living things like the microorganisms that cause botulism. Scorpions, as well as some snakes and spiders, also make toxins. The standard treatment for exposure to a toxin is antitoxin gamma globulins administered immediately by injection. Antitoxin is composed of antibodies against a specific toxin. Most commercial antitoxin is made from the blood of animals such as horses and cows. For example, a very small amount of botulism toxin can be injected into the blood of a horse. In response, the horse's immune system makes antibodies against the toxin. These antibodies can be removed from the horse's blood and given to a patient suffering from botulism. Injected antitoxins protect a patient for a few weeks from the damage that can be done by a toxin. In that time the patient's immune system has an opportunity to heal any

Rattlesnakes are "milked" of their toxic poison so the substance can be used to make antitoxin.

damage done by the toxin. Eventually toxins in blood are metabolized and excreted.

No vaccine presently exists to prevent a person from acquiring HIV and later developing AIDS. Because there is no treatment for AIDS, a vaccine would be especially valuable. Dozens of vaccines have been tested and failed. Problems with the HIV vaccine are similar to problems with a cold vaccine: The virus that causes each of these diseases mutates often. By the time a vaccine against one strain is developed, a different strain has appeared.

Fighting Against Rejection of Organ Transplants

Protection from disease through vaccination is just one of the reasons scientists look for ways to trick the human immune system and prevent it from creating uncomfortable symptoms. Scientists are also researching ways to prevent the body from rejecting a transplanted tissue or organ. Organ transplants are relatively new procedures. For some people who have fatal diseases, they are the only hope. For example, many patients who have lost their kidney function wait for years to receive a new kidney. While they wait, they must go to a kidney dialysis center three or four times a week so that a machine can do the job that their kidneys can no longer perform: remove wastes from blood. In the United States, about eleven thousand kidneys are transplanted each year. Amazingly, 90 percent of those come from living donors, often a relative of the person with the kidney disease.

When the cells of an organ donor are introduced into the body of an organ recipient, the recipient's immune system goes into action. It identifies these cells on the transplanted organ as nonself, and therefore treats them like invaders. As a result the recipient's immune system attempts to destroy the foreign cells. In the past, many organ transplants were unsuccessful because the donor's tissues were rejected by the recipient's immune system.

Fortunately, scientific research over the last fifty years has helped ease rejection of transplanted organs and tissues. Nowadays transplants are usually successful because scientists have discovered ways to suppress the body's natural tendency to reject foreign cells. Immunosuppressant medications that interfere with or prevent the recipient's immune response have been crucial in transplants. Even so, one or two more episodes of rejection typically occur soon after surgery. Another episode may occur three to four months after surgery. Rejection can cause fluid retention, fever, swelling, and tenderness in the area of the transplanted organ. Rejection can usually be stopped by increasing doses of medications that suppress the immune system. Most transplant patients must take these medications for the rest of their lives. Transplanted kidneys can function for thirty years, and recipients usually lead normal, active lives.

Good and Bad Effects of Immunosuppressants

Immunosuppressants were developed by scientists to repress the immune system after a transplant. These drugs work by preventing white blood cells in the recipient's immune system from making antibodies that could destroy the new organ or tissue. These drugs are very good at squelching the rejection process fueled by the immune system. However, they are very expensive and take a heavy toll on the recipient's body.

Immunosuppressant drugs such as cyclosporine A and corticosteroids also can cause weight gain, swelling, nausea, dizziness, depression, thinning of the skin, and lowered resistance to germs. The greatest concern to doctors is that infections can develop easily in patients while their immune systems are on hold. The effect of suppression is so great that even simple viral or bacterial diseases can kill the transplant recipient. Organ recipients also are more prone to cancer and osteoporosis when they are taking these drugs. Immunosuppressant drugs must be continued for the entire lifetime of the patient. Doctors are faced with the challenge of finding the dosage that prevents rejection but does not destroy the body's ability to fight disease.

Liver and Heart Transplants

Kidney dialysis can keep people who have lost their kidney function alive until a kidney is available for transplant, but organ transplant is the only hope for a person with a failed liver. The success rate for liver transplants is a little lower than it is for kidney transplants; even so, about 75 percent of recipients live for at least one year. Liver recipients must take immunosuppressant medications both before and after surgery.

Heart transplantion is one of the newest accomplishments in medicine. This complex surgical procedure is reserved for people with serious types of heart disease who cannot be treated with medication. In some cases, mechanical heart machines keep patients alive for months as they wait for an appropriate donor heart. The need for donor hearts is so great that most patients die while waiting. For those who do receive transplants, immunosuppressant medications are a critical part of recovery.

Bone Marrow Transplants

When a person undergoes an organ transplant, drugs must be used to keep the body from rejecting the new organ.

Bone marrow transplants offer hope to patients on multiple fronts. At first used only to treat blood cancer and tumors of the bone, bone marrow transplants now help patients with other diseases rebuild a population of normal, healthy cells. These new treatments rely on bone marrow because it is a valuable source of stem cells, or starter-type cells, that can develop into cells fulfilling any function.

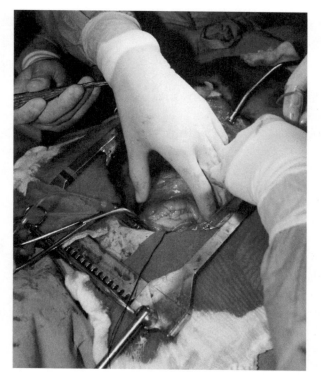

As cancer patients receive their treatments, many normal cells are destroyed along with the cancer cells. By removing bone marrow from a cancer patient before damaging radiation therapy and chemotherapy begin, doctors can obtain a supply of stem cells that can be reinjected into the patient when the cancer-killing treatments have ended.

Bone marrow transplant material that comes from a donor, on the other hand, must be tested carefully to ensure a very close match between donor and recipient. There is a double danger in bone marrow transplant.

Doctors have to worry about rejection plus the donor's mature T cells. Mature T cells of the donor's bone marrow will sometimes attack the recipient's immune system in an attempt to destroy the bone marrow cells. This is such a serious problem that until recently bone marrow transplant material could come only from the patient or from his or her identical twin. And of course the chances that a person with bone marrow cancer will have an identical twin are slim. Today, however, researchers have developed a procedure that uses chemicals to cleanse the donor's bone marrow of the dangerous T cells before the transplant takes place. Immunosuppressant drugs are given to the recipient after surgery to suppress rejection.

Matching Tissues

Scientists have always known that the most successful transplants occur when the tissues of the donor and the recipient are very similar in composition. Each person's cells carry unique molecules that serve as cell markers. Studies have shown that the more closely matched the cell markers of donor and recipient, the more likely it is that the organ will not be rejected. Scientists have discovered that the differences in these cell markers are genetic. So people who are related to each other often have similar molecules on their cell membranes. That is why the most successful transplants occur between identical twins. The next most successful transplants occur between other blood relatives. The majority of surgeons will not consider doing a transplant operation unless there is a 75 percent match between cell markers of the donor and recipient. The chances of two unrelated people having a 100 percent match of cell markers is about one in one hundred thousand. Doctors compare the cell markers on donor and recipient tissues through a complex set of tests. Once a sufficient donor and recipient match has been established, the operation is scheduled.

Compared to complicated surgical procedures required for organ transplant, bone marrow transplant is relatively simple. While the donor is under anesthesia, the doctor removes marrow from the hip bone with a long syringe. This marrow is then injected into the recipient's vein. In the recipient, the marrow travels to bone and takes up residence there. The bone marrow cells begin to divide and eventually replace all of the lost marrow.

Diabetes in the Future

Scientists are looking for ways to help cure diabetes through transplant procedures, and indeed advances in transplant techniques are on the horizon. In one type of diabetes, for example, insulin production is inadequate because the pancreatic cells are not functioning properly. Scientists are exploring ways to transplant these cells, called beta cells, from a healthy person to a diabetic one. Presently the immune system of the recipient will attack and kill the new healthy beta cells. Scientists are working on a technique that removes the part of the beta cells that activates an adverse immune response. In addition to chemically shaving away unwanted cell components, they are researching ways to put healthy beta cells in capsules no wider than a human hair. These capsules would be programmed to let insulin out and blood sugar in without triggering the immune response. Perfecting this transplant is years away, but has lots of potential for helping diabetics in the future.

Genetic Engineering

Scientists are searching for treatments to many immunological diseases through genetic engineering. In gene therapy, genes from one type of organism are removed and combined with genes from another organism. This adds new genes to diseased tissues, ideally enabling them to produce the component that is missing in their systems. Scientists hope that one day the tissue that produces insulin can be genetically changed so that it will manufacture its own protective protein coat. This new "super tissue" could escape destruction when transplanted into the pancreas of a diabetic.

Some forms of gene therapy have already been tried with humans. In 1997 researchers with the National Institute of

Allergy and Infectious Diseases (NIAID) devised a gene therapy to treat the immune disease called chronic granulomatous disease (CGD). This condition disables the immune system's ability to fight off certain fungi and bacteria, leaving the body prone to serious illnesses. The white blood cells of people with CGD cannot make the enzymes responsible for killing bacteria and fungi in their body. Researchers with the NIAID removed stem cells from five people with CGD. Then, taking advantage of the ability of stem cells to develop into any type of cell, the researchers inserted genes that produce the needed enzymes into the stem cells. These corrected cells were reinjected into the patients, whose immune system soon began to function normally. Even though there are problems yet to be solved with this technique, it holds promise for treating many immune system diseases in the future.

Hybridoma Technology

Through a new technique known as hybridoma technology, scientists can obtain large quantities of chemicals that are secreted by cells of the immune system such as antibodies and complement proteins. This ready supply of previously difficult to obtain materials has revolutionized medicine.

A hybridoma is made by fusing two different cells inside one cell membrane. The cells most often selected for fusing are a cell from the immune system and a cancerous cell. Cancer cells are valuable in this research because they are extremely long-lived. The hybrid cell that results can be cloned to produce millions of identical cells. If the original cell secretes antibodies, then all of the clones do also.

One of the first hybridomas created in the lab consisted of a B cell and a cancerous cell. Millions of clones from this hybrid B/cancerous cell secreted a huge quantity of antibodies. Such monoclonal antibodies, as these products are called, have created new ways to prevent and treat disease. It is possible to attach radioactive molecules to monoclonal antibodies. One use of such tagged antibodies is to locate B cells and T cells in the blood of AIDS patients. The radioactive tags

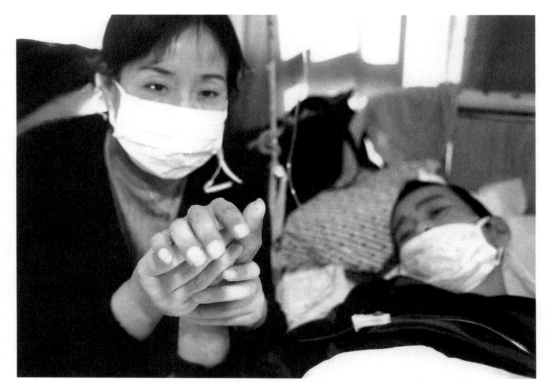

Stem cell research is being conducted in China to find cures for diseases like this patient's leukemia.

enable scientists to follow the antibodies as they move through a blood sample. When they attach themselves to the target cells, scientists can count the number of target cells that are surrounded by radioactive tags. This information helps physicians access the effects of immunosuppressant medications. In a similar way, monoclonal antibodies are being used to track down cancer cells. They can even be linked to anticancer drugs for treatment.

Wrapping Up the Immune System

An invisible army of cells and chemicals called the immune system works around the clock to prevent infection. Made up of tissues scattered throughout the body, this system is responsible for recognizing invaders. It does so by distinguishing normal body cells, or self, from foreign cells, nonself. When nonself cells are found, it is the immune system's job to destroy them. The work of the immune system keeps most people from dying the first time they encounter an infectious agent.

Sometimes the immune system makes mistakes. It can accidentally identify a harmless particle such as dust or pollen as a source of danger. An immune attack against such common materials results in allergies. Another, more dangerous, error is to falsely identify self cells as nonself. When this happens certain parts of the body are treated as intruders and attacked. This type of immune mistake results in autoimmune diseases like lupus and rheumatoid arthritis.

The immune system's ability to correctly identify and destroy nonself cells presents medical science with both opportunities and problems. In the development of vaccines science has found a way to trick the immune system and take advantage of its talents. Vaccines are made from disabled infectious organisms that impersonate infections by microbes and trigger the immune system to make antibodies. Even though vaccines present little or no danger, the body responds to them by creating immunity. Therefore, vaccines provide a way to fight illnesses by preventing them. They are one of the greatest achievements in public health.

On the other hand, the immune system's ability to recognize nonself cells is a problem during cell and organ transplants. In the past, potentially lifesaving transplant surgeries have often failed because the recipient's body rejected the transplanted organ. Traditionally, powerful immunosuppressants have been used in the attempt to prevent rejection, despite the harm these drugs inevitably do to the patient. Investigators today are exploring promising avenues of research with the goal of providing better options in the future.

GLOSSARY

active immunity: Immunity in the body that results from stimulation of disease-causing organisms or vaccines.

allergen: A type of antigen that causes allergy.

allergy: A harmful response of the immune system to a harmless antigen.

antibody: Molecule produced by a B cell in response to an antigen; also called an immunoglobulin.

antigen: A substance that is recognized by the immune system as foreign or nonself; can be a bacterium, virus, protozoan, fungus, or chemical.

autoimmune disease: A condition in which the immune system mistakenly attacks its own body cells.

B cell: A type of lymphocyte that produces antibodies.

beta cells: A type of cell found in the pancreas that manufactures insulin.

bone marrow: Tissues located in the cavities of bones that are the source of all blood cells.

compatibility/incompatibility: Terms expressing the degree of similarity between a donor and a recipient's cells and therefore a measure of how likely the donor cells are to stimulate an immune response in the recipient.

complement: A group of proteins that work together to enhance the function of immune system cells.

hybridoma: A hybrid cell created by fusing a cell from the immune system with a cancer cell used in medicine and research to track cell populations or deliver medications.

immune response: Reaction of the immune system to a foreign substance.

immunosuppressant drug: Medication that prevents the immune system from attacking and destroying transplanted tissue.

inflammatory response: Redness, warmth, swelling, and pain produced in response to infection.

leukocytes: All white blood cells.

lymph: Clear fluid that carries lymphocytes, bathes tissues, and drains lymphatic vessels.

lymphatic vessels: A network of vessels similar to blood vessels that carry lymph.

lymph node: Small organs of the immune system that are distributed around the body.

lymphocyte: A type of white blood cell of the immune system.

macrophage: A type of white blood cell that consumes and kills infectious agents.

monoclonal antibodies: Antibodies made from a single cell or clones of that cell, specific to an antigen.

passive immunity: Immunity in the body that results from the transfer of antibodies from another individual.

pollen count: The density of pollen in the air.

T cell: A type of lymphocyte that coordinates and directs many immune system functions.

toxin: Poison produced by some bacteria, plants, and animals that are harmful to cells.

vaccine: A substance made of dead or weakened antigens that is used to stimulate an immune response to those antigens.

FOR FURTHER READING

Books

Elizabeth Fong, *Body Structures and Functions.* St. Louis, MO: Times Mirror/Mosby Publishers, 1987. Provides simple and thorough descriptions of various diseases of the human body.

Alma Guinness, *ABC's of the Human Body.* Pleasantville, NY: Reader's Digest Association, 1987. Discusses the various structures of the human body and addresses some interesting reasons for certain body functions.

The Handy Science Answer Book. Canton, MI: Visible Ink Press, 1997. Gives very cute explanations for a variety of happenings in the science world.

How in the World? Pleasantville, NY: Reader's Digest Association, 1990. This book provides interesting coverage of both physical and biological events that occur in life.

David E. Larson, *Mayo Clinic Family Health Book.* New York: William Morrow, 1996. Describes in simple terms the many diseases that can affect the human body.

Susan McKeever, *The Dorling Kindersley Science Encyclopedia.* New York: Dorling Kindersley, 1994. Gives concise information on physical and biological occurrences in life. Good illustrations help to explain topics.

Mary Lou Mulvihill, *Human Diseases.* Norwalk, CT: Appleton & Lange, 1995. Provides a good description of the most common diseases of the human body.

National Institute of Allergy and Infectious Disease, *Understanding Vaccines.* Bethesda, MD: National Institute of Health, 1998. Easy to use reference book that explains how vaccines are made and why they are important.

World Book Medical Encyclopedia. Chicago: World Book, 1995. Provides a vast amount of information on physiology of the human body systems.

Internet Sources

Steve Beach, "How Allergies Work," 2001. www.howstuffworks.com.

Kevin Bonsor, "How AIDS Works," 2001. www.howstuffworks.com.

Marshall Brain, "How the Immune System Works," 2001. www. howstuffworks.com.

James B. Caress and Glynn P. Hyde, "Myasthenia Gravis," 2001. www.wfubmc.edu.

Websites

About (www.about.com). Easy to use site that offers information on all topics, including health and medicine.

Countdown for Kids Magazine (www.jdf.org). Students can research any topics that interest them, including health and medicine.

Fact Monster, Learningnetwork (www.factmonster.com). Provides information on all topics including a good science encyclopedia; suitable for any student.

MSN Search (www.search.msn.com). Provides a science library suitable for most students.

Yucky Kids (www.nj.com). Access information on all body systems.

WORKS CONSULTED

Books

Robert Berkow, *The Merck Manual of Medical Information*. New York: Pocket Books, 1997. Provides a detailed explanation of all organs. This book gives information on the causes, symptoms, diagnosis, and treatment of many diseases.

Charlotte Dienhart, *Basic Human Anatomy and Physiology*. Philadelphia: W.B. Saunders, 1979. This textbook covers the structure and function of all organ systems in the human body. It also provides information on symptoms and treatments of various diseases.

William C. Goldberg, *Clinical Physiology Made Ridiculously Simple*. Miami, FL: Med Masters, 1995. This booklet gives a very detailed explanation of body systems. Illustrations reinforce the written content.

John Hole Jr., *Essentials of Human Anatomy and Physiology*. Dubuque, IA: Wm. C. Brown, 1992. This textbook of anatomy and physiology provides detailed explanations of the structure and function of all human body systems.

Anthony L. Komaroff, *Harvard Medical School Family Health Guide*. New York: Simon & Schuster, 1999. This book provides comprehensive coverage of the various disorders and diseases that can affect the human body. Symptoms, causes, diagnoses, and treatment options are provided.

Ann Kramer, *The Human Body, The World Book Encyclopedia of Science*. Chicago: World Book, 1987. Provides information on all body systems as well as explanations about unusual and interesting events that occur in the human body.

Stanley Loeb, *The Illustrated Guide to Diagnostic Tests*. Springhouse, PA: Springhouse, 1994. This medical book gives a very thorough description and explanation of how and why medical technologies are employed to diagnose and treat human diseases and disorders.

Elaine Marieb, *Human Anatomy and Physiology*. Redwood City, CA: Benjamin/Cummings, 1995. Offers a very detailed explanation of all human body structures and organs.

U.S. Department of Health and Human Services, *Systemic Lupus Erythematosus*. Bethesda, MD: National Institute of Health, February 2000. Written for people who have SLE or lupus, this book is easy to understand and answers a lot of questions.

―――, *Understanding Autoimmune Diseases*. Bethesda, MD: National Institute of Health, May 1998. An introduction to autoimmune diseases written for the layman.

―――, *Understanding the Immune System*. Bethesda, MD: National Institute of Health, January 1993. A good resource for general information on how the immune system works, and research done in genetic engineering.

Internet Sources

Centers for Disease Control and Prevention, "How do Vaccines Work?" *CDC*, 2001. www.cdc.gov.

Shane T. Grey, "Genetic Engineering and Xenotransplantation," *Actionbioscience.org*, 2001. www.actionbioscience.org.

The Human Internet, "Understanding the Immune System," 2001. www.allergies.about.com.

Merck, "Infectious Diseases and Immune Response," *Merck Manual*, 2001. www.merck.com.

National Institute of Allergy and Infectious Diseases, "Inappropriate Immune Response in Inner City Kids," *NIAID NetNews*, 2001. www.niaid.nih.gov.

Websites

American Autoimmune Related Diseases Association (www.aarda.org). Explains the immune system and gives descriptions of diseases related to it. Also contains articles from "InFocus" newsletter about autoimmune diseases.

CDC (www.cdc.gov). Information from the Centers for Disease Control and Prevention on any topic in health. Includes good articles on the importance of childhood immunizations and problems due to antibiotic resistance.

Clinical Implications (www.nobel.se). Contains drawings and photographs along with information on all medical topics.

Cornell Medical College (www.edcenter.med.cornell.edu). The medical college of Cornell provides a wide range of information on body systems.

11th Hour (www.blackwellscience.com). Great teacher resource for any type of information in science. To find information on the immune system, go to "Introduction to Biology."

JAMA HIV/AIDS Resource Center (www.ama-assn.org). The *Journal of the American Medical Association,* published by the American Medical Association, is a great resource for any topic in medicine.

Merck Manual (www.merck.com). This website gives a detailed explanation of diseases.

NIAID NetNews (www.niaid.nih.gov). Information provided by the National Institute of Allergy and Infectious Diseases covers a variety of immunological topics. Excellent article on antimicrobial resistance.

INDEX

acetylcholine, 62–63
acquired immunity, 22–23
acquired immunodeficiency syndrome (AIDS), 31, 34–38, 75, 81
AIDS. *See* acquired immunodeficiency syndrome
allergies
    causes of, 41–42
    origin of term, 52
    symptoms of, 47
    testing for, 45–46
    treatments for, 49–50
    types of, 44–45, 47–52
allergists, 45–46
ANA. *See* antinuclear antibody test
anaphylaxis, 45, 49
anemia, 58
antibodies
    attacks on encapsulated extracellular bacteria by, 29
    description of, 13
    gamma globulins, 73–74
    immune responses caused by, 14–15
    immunoglobulin E (IgE), 42
    in newborns, 22–23
    roles of, in allergic reactions, 50–51
antigens
    description of, 10
    gaining immunity against, 23
    how immune system protects the body against
        attacks on extracellular bacteria, 27–29

        attacks on intracellular bacteria, 30
        inflammation, 25–27
    neutralization of, 13–14
    types of, 30
antihistamines, 50
antinuclear antibody test (ANA), 57
antitoxins, 15, 74–75
asthma, 49
autoimmune diseases
    causes of, 53–55
    types of
        diabetes mellitus, 65–66, 80
        multiple sclerosis, 60–62
        myasthenia gravis, 62–63
        psoriasis, 64–65
        rheumatoid arthritis, 57–60
        systemic lupus erythematosus, 55–57

bacteria, 27–30
basophils, 18, 42–44
B cells, 13–15, 23–24, 28–29, 42–43, 81
beta cells, 80
birth control pills, 57
blood, 26–27
blood transfusions, 36
bone marrow, 13, 58
bone marrow transplants, 78–80
breast-feeding, 36

cancer, 34, 38, 77–78, 81
CDC. *See* Centers for Disease Control and Prevention

cell markers, 79
cells
    antigens, description of, 10
    B, 13–15, 23–24, 28–29, 42–43, 81
    basophils, 42–44
    beta, 80
    lymph, 12–16
    mast, 42–44
    memory, 14, 23
    natural killer, 16–17
    plasma, 13–14
    stem, 13, 78, 81
    T, 15–16, 30, 32–34, 53, 79, 81
    viruses in, 30
    white blood
        granulocytes, 17–18
        lymphocytes, 13–17, 23–24
        monocytes, 18–20
Centers for Disease Control and
    Prevention (CDC), 36–37
CGD. See chronic granulomatous
    disease
chemicals, 38
chemotherapy, 38
chronic granulomatous disease
    (CGD), 81
cilia, 12
colds, 37
complement system, 19–20
corticosteroids, 63, 77
cyclosporine A, 77
cytokines, 15–16, 30

dander, 47
diabetes mellitus, 65–66, 80
dialysis, 77
dirt, 10
disease-modifying antiheumatic
    drugs (DMARDs), 59

DMARDs. See disease-modifying
    antiheumatic drugs
drug allergies, 48–49
drugs, 38
DTP vaccines, 71
dust allergies, 47–48

E. coli, 27–28
encapsulated extracellular bacteria,
    28–29
eosinophils, 18
epinephrine, 50
erythrocyte sedimentation rate
    (ESR), 57, 59
ESR. See erythrocyte sedimenta-
    tion rate
estrogen, 57
extracellular bacteria, 27–29

fasting glucose, 66
FDA. See Food and Drug
    Administration
flu, 30, 37
food allergies, 48–49
Food and Drug Administration
    (FDA), 71

gamma globulins, 73–74
gene therapy, 80–81
glucose, 65–66
granulomas, 27–28
granulocytes, 17–18

heart transplants, 77–78
helper T cells, 32–34
hepatitis, 49
histamines, 18, 43–44, 50–51
HIV. See human immunodeficien-
    cy virus
hives, 44, 49

hormone replacement therapy, 57
human immunodeficiency virus
    (HIV), 31–33, 37–38, 75
hybridoma technology, 81–82
hydrophobia, 74

IgE. *See* immunoglobulin E
immune system
    methods used for protecting the
        body
        attacks on extracellular bacte-
            ria by, 27–29
        attacks on intracellular bacte-
            ria by, 30
        inflammation, 25–27
    roles of, 8–12
immunity, 22–23
immunization, 69
immunoglobulin E (IgE), 42, 44,
    46, 50
immunosuppressants, 77
infections, causes of, 8–9
inflammation, 18, 25–27, 44,
    61–62
influenza. *See* flu
injections, 49–50, 71, 74
insects, 37
insulin, 65, 80
interferon, 16
intracellular bacteria, 30

Jenner, Edward, 69
juvenile diabetes, 65

Kaposi's sarcoma, 34
kissing, 37

leukocytes, 27
liver transplants, 77–78
lumbar puncture, 62

lupus. *See* systemic lupus erythe-
    matosus
lymph cells, 12–16
lymph nodes, 20–22
lymphocytes
    B cell, 13–15, 23–24, 28–29,
        42–43, 81
    natural killer cells, 16–17
    T cell, 15–16, 30, 32–34, 53,
        79, 81
lymphoid organs, 11
lymphomas, 34
lysosomes, 17

macrophages, 18–20, 27, 29
magnetic resonance imaging
    (MRI), 61–62
malnutrition, 38
marrow. *See* bone marrow
mast cells, 42–44
measles, 71
memory cells, 14, 23
microbes, 23, 72
mites, 47
MMR vaccines, 71
molds, 47–48
monocytes, 18–20
mosquitoes, 37–38
mouth, 12
MRI. *See* magnetic resonance
    imaging
MS. *See* multiple sclerosis
mucus, 12
multiple sclerosis (MS), 60–62
myasthenia gravis, 62–63
myelin, 62

National Institute of Allergy and
    Infectious Diseases (NIAID),
    80–81

natural killer cells, 16–17
nerve conduction test, 62
neutrophils, 18–19
NIAID. *See* National Institute of Allergy and Infectious Diseases
non–organ-specific autoimmune diseases, 55
nonsteroidal anti-inflammatory drugs (NSAIDs), 57, 59
nose, 12
NSAIDs. *See* nonsteroidal anti-inflammatory drugs

organ-specific autoimmune diseases, 55
organ transplants, rejections of, 76–77
osteoporosis, 77

parasites, 18
passive immunity, 22–23
peanuts, 48
penicillin, 49
perennial allergic rhinitis, 47
Peyer's patches, 22
phagocytosis, 17
phototherapy, 65
plaques, 61–62
plasma cells, 13–14
poison ivy, 52
poison oak, 52
poisons, 15
polio, 71
proteins, complement, 19–20
pseudopod, 17
psoriasis, 64–65

RA. *See* rheumatoid arthritis
rabies, 73–74
radiation, 38

radioallergosorbent (RAST) blood tests, 46
rashes, 48–49
RAST. *See* radioallergosorbent blood tests
red pulp, 22
rheumatoid arthritis (RA), 57–60
roundworms, 18

saliva, 12
scars, 27
scorpions, 74
scratch tests, 45–46
sex, 36
shellfish, 48
shots. *See* injections
skin, 11–12
SLE. *See* systemic lupus erythematosus
smallpox, 69
spiders, 74
spleen, 22, 38
splinters, 10
stem cells, 13, 78, 81
stomach, 12
streptococci, 14, 29
sulfa drugs, 49
sweat, 38
swelling, 27
swimming, 38
systemic lupus erythematosus (SLE), 55–57

TB. *See* tuberculosis
T cells, 15–16, 30, 32–34, 53, 79, 81
tears, 12, 38
thymus, 15
toilet seats, 38
tonsils, 22

transplants
    bone marrow, 78–80
    liver and heart, 77–78
    rejection of, 76–77
    to cure diabetes, 80
tuberculosis (TB), 28, 52
Type I allergic reactions, 44–45
Type II allergic reaction, 50–51
Types III and IV allergic reactions,
    51–52

vaccines
    history of, 68–69
    problems with making, 72–73
    reactions to, 70–71
    roles of, 70
    types of

antitoxins, 74–75
DTP and MMR, 71
for preventing organ trans-
    plant rejections, 76–77
gamma globulins, 73–74
viruses
    acquired immunodeficiency
        syndrome, 31, 34–38
    in cells, 30
    human immunodeficiency,
        31–33, 37–38

white blood cells
    granulocytes, 17–18
    lymphocytes, 13–18
    monocytes, 18–20
white pulp, 22

PICTURE CREDITS

ABOUT THE AUTHORS

Both Pam Walker and Elaine Wood have degrees in biology and education from colleges in Georgia. They have taught science in grades seven through twelve since the mid-1980s. Ms. Walker and Ms. Wood are coauthors of more than a dozen science-teacher resource activity books and two science textbooks.